# Smarter: It's Something You Become

## Table of Contents

*This book is dedicated to Superintendent Cliff Janey, Newark Public Schools, and the administrators, teachers, and parents who support and celebrate the high intellectual performance of the student authors of this book.*

A publication of the National Urban Alliance for Effective Education (NUA) by and for the students of the Newark Public Schools, Newark, NJ

# Foreword

This is the second year in a row that students from the Newark Public Schools were invited to express their thoughts and feelings about themselves and about important events in their lives, this time inspired by the theme "Smarter: It's Something You Become."

Children do not come to school with a fixed amount of intelligence that determines how well they will succeed as they move through the grades. Instead, their intelligence is developed, nurtured, and increased by a variety of experiences, including the effective instruction they receive in school. The modifiability of intelligence is a core NUA belief, grounded in the knowledge that each individual has untapped potential for high intellectual performance.

Newark teachers, collaborating with NUA mentors, daily translate that belief into action. What topics and activities will most engage students? What strategies will make the learning substantive and memorable? What will help students understand deeply and be able to represent their learning in interesting, thoughtful, and creative ways? These questions drive the educators' instructional decisions as they move students towards higher levels of performance.

The works in this book reveal the lively, creative response students make to such effective instruction. Each essay, poem, story, or work of art reveals a delightful individual who is becoming ever more confident and competent.

In line with the theme of *becoming*, we invited a special guest to contribute the lead piece in this collection. Andrea Wise writes of her travel in Senegal, reflecting on the insights she gained along the way. We see her journey not only as a fascinating actual experience but also as a metaphor for the life journeys in which the students of the Newark Public Schools are engaged.

Feature Writer Matthew Lichten offers an inspiring reflection on his work as a teacher who is doing much to enrich his students' life journeys. His thoughts are representative of the commendable efforts of the teachers of the Newark Public Schools, and his statement is a fitting lead to the Adult Contributions section, which includes writing and artwork from teachers, administrators, and NUA mentors.

NUA is pleased once again to help students make their voices heard with this publication. We hope it will inspire others who are engaged in their own life journeys.

Yvette Jackson
Chief Executive Officer, NUA

# Introduction

We believe that student voices must be added to the education reform movement underway in the United States. Students, who are most affected by education policy, must be embraced as partners in the education system if we are to reverse underachievement. This volume contains the voices of students and the adults who work with them—the emotions, hopes, dreams, and spirits that can help to define humankind as they reveal the potential of each individual.

When teachers engage students in relevant and meaningful thinking, they foster the potential that defines our true destiny: "Each person bears a uniqueness that asks to be lived." How successful we will be in fulfilling that destiny is determined by how well we can connect with the deeper intellectual, emotional, and spiritual resources that influence the people we will become. The voices in this book are unique, framed by the creativity and deep thinking the students bring to their learning. Their expressions through prose, poetry, and art show their high intellectual performance. These are anchored by their teachers' high expectations that all will graduate successfully prepared to enter an institution of higher education, the workplace, and the arena of lifelong learning.

These students and their teachers have dared to initiate education reform one student, one classroom, and one building at a time. They are engaged in fearless learning and teaching that empowers them as individuals and as a learning community. They illustrate the truth of John Quincy Adams's words: "Patience and perseverance have a magical effect before which difficulties disappear and obstacles vanish."

The students in Newark, NJ, get up every morning eager to learn, to express themselves, and to find their destiny. In a sense, the students are saying to the teachers: "Believe in me and help me reach my true potential!"

Educators in Newark, NJ, get up every morning with the belief that they can dramatically alter the life trajectories of their students. Their passion and commitment guide them as they give their students the gift of learning and the firm belief that all students can achieve the highest levels of performance. In a sense, the teachers are saying to their students: "Shoot for the moon. Even if you miss, you land among the stars."

This collection shines a bright light of recognition on the God-given capacity and potential of the writers and artists who are part of the Newark Public Schools. NUA salutes them!

Eric J. Cooper
President and Founder, NUA

# La Chaleur
## Andrea Wise, Guest Writer

It's so hot here.

(La Chaleur means The Heat, and that and sand seem to be the two main things Matam has an abundance of, it being the desert and all. And I guess there are a lot of goats, too. This is the first of occasional mass emails to all you wonderful people on my musings from Senegal.)

On Saturday we made the ten-hour journey from Dakar to Matam, which included a lunch detour in St. Louis, the former capital of Senegal. The "we" included a UNFPA driver, me, Mala (another New School student) and our two "binomes." Our projects here have been structured such that we are each paired with a Senegalese student from the Institute for Population, Development and Reproductive Health and the University Cheikh Anta Diop in Dakar, thus each of us has a "binome" or pair. Mine is named Latsouk and he's awesome. We are both really interested in migration. He wrote his master's thesis on urban refugees in Dakar, and he wears Sebagos with Lacoste polo shirts. So as an added plus, I like his style. Needless to say we get along really well, and for this I am extremely grateful. Here in Matam the strength of my experience so far is in fact the congenial and joke-cracking rapport of "L'equipe Matam," which is good because we spend a LOT of time together and in very close quarters. Mala's binome Ngone in particular is hilaaaaarious and has me hysterically laughing all the time. So far we have been working at the UNFPA office finalizing our field projects. Latsouk and I are investigating why the contraception prevalence rate in this region is so low and will be conducting interviews and focus groups looking at the roles/impacts of religion, migration, and socio-cultural factors on attitudes towards family planning and contraception use.

But back to the heat. When we arrived at 6:30 pm on Saturday it was 108. It has gotten up to 122 during the day, and there really isn't much else I can say except the heat is all-consuming. We are in the rainy season, but the rains are late this year. They should have started a couple of weeks ago. When I return to Dakar at the end of July, the hills should be green with foliage. I don't think much flora grows here in Matam, but the break from the heat is greatly anticipated by all. Really all you can do is adapt, drink as much water as possible, appreciate any second spent in air conditioning, and hope the electricity stays on (which it does most, but certainly not all of the time). I'm still figuring out how to describe Matam since I haven't been here very long, but I will say right now that it is very remote, the climate is very harsh, and it is very poor.

My time in Dakar already seems so long ago. I was there for the first 9 days of my trip with the first 4 essentially being vacation. I was able to see a lot of the city, including going to Goree Island, and Dakar is a wonderful place to visit. In fact, life there felt pretty easy for me, in that way, where if you have the ways (as all of us students do, relatively speaking) then the means are so much more unencumbered.

Some other things worth noting:

- The cow in our yard gave birth the other day, so now we have a baby cow.
- I speak French almost exclusively, and am trying to pick up some Wolof.
- I see Mauritania every day (a country some of you know I am slightly obsessed with) as we live a few blocks from the Senegal River, which is the border between Senegal and Mauritania. The way lives are lived at and on a river is new and fascinating to me. We have a plan to take a trip across next weekend.

- My diet is fairly balanced here, with pretty equal portions meat (fish, beef or mutton), carbs (couscous or rice), and vegetables (carrots, cabbage, eggplant, okra, yams, and potatoes) at every lunch and dinner.
- Mala and I are the only foreigners we've seen so far in Matam. Little kids yell "TOUBAB!" (which means foreigner/white person) and point at us and then come up with their arms extended to shake our hand.

There have been a fair share of bumps on this journey, some significant, but I will not get into any of that now, mostly because it's not what is really important. My excitement for this trip and this project have not once wavered. In coming from the fatigue and stress of NYC what struck me squarely during my first days in Dakar was being able to slow down and simply recognize the fact that I am breathing and that I am alive. These are things I know I used to be much more conscious of and intentional about and thus things I hope to regain and maintain once I return.

A couple photos from Matam are attached.

I hope you all are fantastic,
Andrea

A binôme: Guest Writer, Andrea, and her colleague, Latsouk. Latsouk is a Senegalese student from the Institute for Population, Development and Reproductive Health and the University Cheikh Anta Diop in Dakar.

# Smarter: Grade 6 Contributors

## The Wheel Of Intelligence

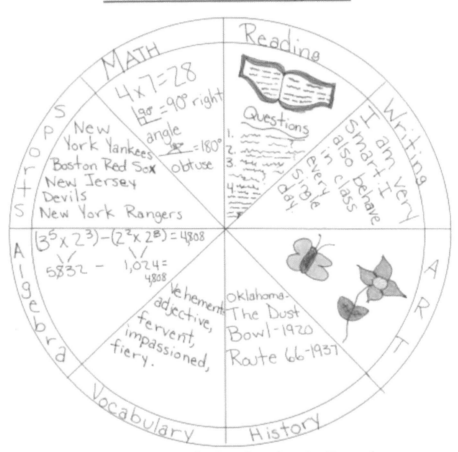

Made By: Stephanie Guambana

## Hello Citizens of the World

How I became smart was by going to school and showing the teachers that I have good behavior and strong attention skills. If you pay attention in class, it will help you develop your brain. As you go from grade to grade, you grow smarter by learning new things.

My favorite subject is social studies because you learn about different people and places. You also learn about history. It makes me have more to talk about and write about.

I also like science because you learn about plants, space and the human body. By becoming smarter about these things I can make myself healthier as well as the earth where I live.

Shakur Hunt
Dr. E. Alma Flagg School


## Smarter

Smarter
To be!
To hold the key -
Doors open wide
Knowledge inside

The difference between
Wrong
Right
Fact
Opinion

The mind that is Smart
Is a respected temple,
The kingdom of the heart

Life is seen through the mind
So I will forever keep safe
My mind
To be Smarter!

Allondra Silva
Dr. William H. Horton School

# The Loss

Have you ever lost someone you love very much?  Well, I have. It all started on April 11, 2009. I lost someone I loved a lot. He was like a brother to me. He was also like a brother to my brothers, my big brother and my little brother. He was like a son to my mom and dad. They loved him a lot. He was really special to us. I had him for eleven years and my big brother had him for thirteen years. So, just imagine losing someone you love after thirteen years. It's hard. I still cry till this day.

He was a dog: a family dog. He would give me a paw when I needed help. He would save me when I was in trouble. And that is why I loved him so much. He would give me hugs. He would lick my cheek. He would even help my parents. That's how good a dog he was. His name was Apollo. The day he died we took him to the humane society around eight or nine o'clock in the morning. We put him to sleep so he could get out of all the pain. I prayed for him every night and would always wish for him to come back. But it looks like that will never happen. I guess he's gone forever.

My mom always tells me that he is in Heaven watching over me, my family, and my other dog, Anemasis. We've had her for almost three years. Now I know that he is in Heaven watching over me, my family, and my dog. I just wish I could see him and feel his fur one more time and also tell him that I love him one more time.

Shayna Morel
Rafael Hernandez School

# Smarter

S - 	Smart is what got me into 6th grade
M - 	Math is one of my favorite subjects
A - 	Academics is what I do best
R - 	Responsible for reminding myself of things
T - 	To become smart I study every day
E - 	Every day I am on point and focused
R - 	Remembering how to stay smart

Being smart is what is going to take me higher and higher to get a scholarship.

Kendall Barnes
Dr E. Alma Flagg School

## Smart

| S | Scholarships you can earn being smart |
|---|---|
| M | More knowledge each day is becoming smart |
| A | An art of knowing |
| R | Ready to learn |
| T | Terrific people are smart |

Alex Lopez
Hawkins Street School

## Being Smart

If you want to be cool,
You must stay in school.
Math is lots of fun,
It has questions like 1 + 1.
In literacy, you read and write, 19
Throughout the night
Here and there,
It will help you everywhere.
Being smart is like a shopping cart.
Knowledge gathering for me
Takes me on the road where I want to be.

Cristian Navas
Miller Street Academy

## Smarter

Smarter means:

Going to Science High School
Not cutting class
Becoming a lawyer
Taking the right path

Smarter means ME being ME
I am SMARTER; this is the new me.

Destiney Dupree
Dr. E. Alma Flagg School

## Your Secrets Are Not Safe With Me

The loud noise of a car crash spread around the neighborhood. It was Andrew's father in a tragic car accident. His father was all he had left. Now there was no family left for him to go to.

All of Andrew's aunts and uncles were all either deceased or somewhere out of state. Some of them were even out of the country. His mother had died from AIDS. His mother caught AIDS from biting a person with AIDS. She got into a fight with a not so old man. He looked like he was in his late thirties. The man bumped into her. She said something and next thing you know, they were fighting. Not knowing that the man had AIDS, she bit him and she ran.

On the day of the car crash, Andrew was taken out of his old neighborhood and was placed in another one. He was taken away by D.Y.F.S. That night he cried and cried. The next morning, his foster mother, Mrs. Anderson, took him out of his old school and he was placed in a different school. The school seemed well taken care of. Andrew stayed there for a couple of weeks and everything was going fine. He was only in the sixth grade with problems but things were still going good.

Years passed by and things were beginning to change. Everything was changing, all except his two best friends, Samantha and Tamara. They graduated together and went to the same ninth grade high school. And they even told their deepest secrets to each other.

One day in class, Tamara told Andrew and Samantha that she might be transferring. Then at lunch time, Tamara, Andrew, and Samantha all sat at the same lunch table, and without realizing, they started telling stories and secrets about their lives. Tamara went first. Then Samantha went. After that, it was Andrew's turn. He began to speak about his family's deaths and how his mother died from AIDS. Samantha felt sad. On the other hand, Tamara made it seem like she had to leave, so she did.

The next day, everyone stopped talking to Andrew and Samantha. They both wondered why. That morning, Tamara found out that she wasn't transferring. She felt dumb on the inside. She felt dumb because she had gone around the whole school and told everyone how Andrew's mother had AIDS. The part that she didn't tell everyone was how she had died from it. So now, everyone thinks that Andrew's mother has AIDS and there's a chance that Andrew may have it from living in the house with her. Tamara thought that she was transferring and would never see them again.

Andrew and Samantha still wondered why no one was talking to them. Until this one boy came up to them and said, "I hope you don't have AIDS like your mother does; because if you do, then you're not welcome here. And I hope that you don't get addicted to drugs like your mother did." The first time, he was talking about Andrew. But the second time he was talking about Samantha. The boy smiled and ran as fast as he could. Samantha and Andrew started realizing how the boy had found out. There was only one person who could have told him. This was Tamara.

Andrew and Samantha walked past Tamara with anger and embarrassment. "How could you? You told everyone in this school about Andrew and my life stories, which were considered our own secrets. Why would you even think about doing that?" cried Samantha.

Tamara looked around as if she was confused. The next morning, Andrew and Samantha were beginning to be noticeable. Everyone suddenly began to start talking to them again but had stopped talking to Tamara.

For the next couple of days, Tamara tried speaking to Andrew and Samantha but the most response that she got from them was "hello." Other than that, all they did was look at her. The end of the day came finally, and two boys and three girls said "hey" to Samantha and Andrew.

Time went by and Tamara couldn't take it anymore. At lunch, Tamara sat by herself. Moments later, she got up and stood on the table. Everyone looked at her and she began apologizing to Andrew and Samantha. She told everyone in the cafeteria how everything she said was a lie. Andrew and Samantha were in total shock because she got up there in front of everyone and said that. Later on that day, everyone in school began talking to Samantha and Andrew again. Now they all became friends but no more secrets were told to Tamara. Other than that, everything was back to normal. Sometimes, being smarter is more than just being wiser. It can be about being mature and learning how to keep some things to yourself.

Bre-Anne Garrett
Rafael Hernandez School

Tatiana Matias

Miller Street School

## Briana

Do you have a person or family member you admire? I do. Her name is Briana and she is my favorite sister in the whole wide world. She's everything to me—my friend and my sister. We do everything together. I love her with all my heart. There are five reasons why I admire her:

1) She's always there for me just like I'm there for her when she's in trouble.
2) We do everything together.
3) We use each other's phones.
4) We sleep in the same room and we go to the same school.
5) We tell each other everything.

We don't keep anything from each other or to ourselves. We even share tears, when I cry, she cries and when she cries, I cry. I love my sister, Briana, with all my heart and I look up to her. I learn from her. We grow smarter together. I hope and wish we are together until the day we die.

Jaleesa Boney
Rafael Hernandez School

## Be Smarter

If you want to be smarter
Just open a book
If you want to be smarter
Stay in school
Being in school
Helps you learn
Reading will
Help you lead the way

Dennie Molina
(poem and drawing)
McKinley School

### *Pencil*

*Pencil.*

*Pencil is cool.*

*Pencil.*

*We need you to show our wisdom. We sharpen you up.*

*We can write with you.*

*Pencil, oh pencil. You sure sound like bees in a hive when you are in the*

*sharpener.*

David Jimenez
Rafael Hernandez School

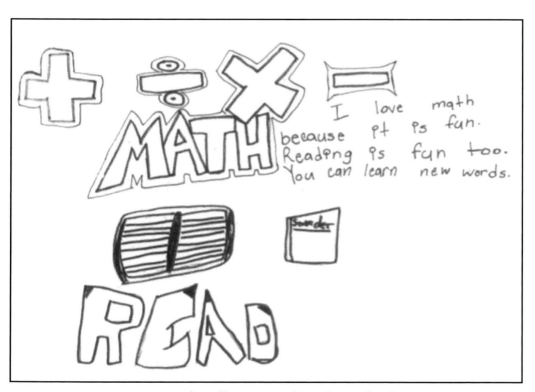

Juan Carlos Ulloa, Dr. E. Alma Flagg School

## Weather Watch

The worst weather I ever saw was when I was nine years old in Santo Domingo. The weather changed so suddenly. It was a tornado!

At first, it was spinning a little. But I didn't know what it was until I saw it begin to rain and I could hear thunder. Then it started to take out trees, bushes, and houses! I realized then that it's true what they say: we do learn from our experiences. Our experiences can make us wiser.

The next thing I knew it was coming towards me. Before long, I woke everyone up. I was worried about me and my brothers and sisters.

After that, we went to the basement. Suddenly, our house went "bye, bye." At that moment we just sat inside the basement.

Finally, after five hours in the basement, my mother went to check if the tornado was over. Once it was over, my mom said we're going back to the United States.

Anien Pilozo
Rafael Hernandez School

## How Are You Smarter?

Every day, when people come to school, we learn new things and that's how you get smarter.

When we were babies, our parents were our teachers and they taught us how to take a bath, eat, walk, talk, and how to brush our teeth. That's another way we get smarter because we learn from the adults around us. Now that we're older, our teachers teach us even more. When we read a book, whether it's a folktale, fiction, or even nonfiction, we still learn and get smarter because it builds up our vocabulary and some books may even build up our imaginations and self-esteem. Asking questions and answering questions also make you get smarter because when you don't understand something, it's better to ask questions. You'll get a better understanding of what you have to do. Another way you get smarter is by listening to what your teachers or parents say.

This is how I get smarter.

Priscilla Fernandez
Miller Street Academy

## Just Imagine

It was a bright sunny day in Thankstown where a 12 year old girl named Crystal was preparing for her Thanksgiving Day family reunion at her house in Canada. She was as excited as a happy face icon. She would be spending the day helping her mother and learning more about cooking for her family.

Crystal was helping her mother this year with the turkey. She was just about to put the turkey in the oven but she heard a sudden noise. She figured it was probably the turkey going "gobble, gobble!!" As she turned around she saw her little brother Steve imitating a turkey. It was very funny.

Just after she put the turkey in, she sat down while eating some pumpkin pie and started to think how Thanksgiving was hundreds of years ago. She started to put all the things she had learned at school together and came to a conclusion. She put her hand on her chin and started to wonder. After five minutes of thinking: POP!! She remembered how Thanksgiving always occurred in November and how the Pilgrims were the first to make this holiday so special.

Soon after, she started to notice her family gathering in. She quickly scurried to the door and greeted and welcomed her family into the house. When she was eating dinner, she started to wonder aloud, "Hmmmmm! Doesn't it feel like back then at the original Thanksgiving?" Just then her grandpa heard her and said, "Yes, but without the funny looking clothes." Everyone chuckled and giggled. It was a wonderful day we were having. I was learning more about cooking, family and the connections they share.

Karina Rivera
Ridge Street School

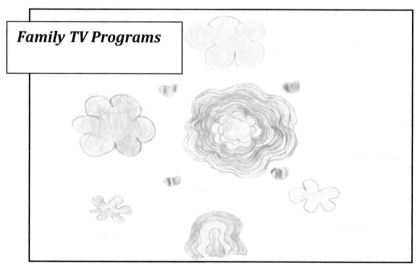

*Family TV Programs*

Kayla Reeves
Dr. William H. Horton School

# The Big *Wave*

When I was eight years old I went to Florida. We had a very big *heat wave* (or at least that's what *I* called it at the time). It was very scary for me because I was only eight years old and my mom was talking to her friend so she didn't see anything that was happening.

"Oh! No!"

At first, I did not see the wave coming because I was playing around and not paying attention. When I turned around I saw it. I was trying to move but I had already gotten wet.

Then my mom saw me soaked and very wet. She asked me what happened. I said, "it was a very big *heat wave*; it splashed me." I got mad because I did not know it was coming my way. If I had known, I would have moved.

After that, we went into a basement because we got scared. We thought it would never go away. Half the town was flooded. I was surprised. I never thought it would happen.

Finally, we heard on the radio that the storm was over. We went back outside and played on the beach. I know better now that a *heat wave* has little to do with water. I am also better about being aware of my surroundings.

Melissa Pinto
Rafael Hernandez School

Kymeasha Selph, Chancellor Avenue School

## Immigration and Friends

My neighborhood is a nice place because immigrants live there. The immigrants in my neighborhood are so nice. They like to share their belongings. They also give food to people. They are so kind they share and care for their friends, family, and neighborhood.

The most important change is that a lot of the immigrants that live here now are from Puerto Rico and lots of other places. It is so important to have more types of people here in our neighborhood. Our neighborhood is a nice place to live.

On the other hand, we live here. But I miss my family in Puerto Rico. I love Puerto Rico so much. I wish that I could go over there or my family could come over here so that they can visit me.

Another important change is that we dance. The Cha-Cha slide to Latino music is a favorite. I like to dance a lot. In our neighborhood, Latinos love to dance a lot. We think it's cool and fun to dance. But for me, it is just fun to dance.

I hope there will be more immigrants coming to my neighborhood in the future. I think my neighborhood is the best place ever to live. The reason I say this is because there are so many things that people may not know. In our neighborhood, we learn from one another because we share parts of our cultures. Lots of people love this neighborhood a lot. They say it's the best neighborhood they have ever been to.

Come and visit us the next time you're in Newark!

Katherine Muñoz
Rafael Hernandez School

Darline Cruz
McKinley School

# My Day at the Football Stadium

On a cold Sunday night, my friends Kevin, Alex and I went to the football game. It was the Jets versus the Chargers. We were having lots of fun. While we were watching the game we got hungry and went for a little snack.

On the way back to our seats, I saw a wonderful play and I stopped in my tracks to watch it. Kein and Alex didn't see me stop. So they kept walking. So I kept watching. When the play was over, I looked up and I didn't see my friends.

I started looking for my friends but I couldn't find them anywhere. I stopped for a second and started thinking about where I might find them. Then I had an idea where I could find them. So I went to the shop where they sell snacks to see if they were there. They weren't there. Then I smacked myself on the head as I realized that they could be back at our seats. I went back to where we were sitting and I saw them. I sat down in my seat and finished watching the game. I said to myself, "I feel so smart right now."

David Nunez
Rafael Hernandez School

Aiyana Sanabria
Dr. E. Alma Flagg School

## My Day at the Stadium

There was this one day when I went to see a baseball game. It was the best game I've ever been to (even though my team, the Bears, was losing to Tampa). It was the second inning and the score was six to three. I was mad because when it got to the eighth inning the score was eight to five. But when it hit the ninth inning, the batter from the Bears was up.

Sandy hit a flyer. The bases were loaded. When he hit that ball the guys from the other team were scrambling to get the ball but they were too slow. Everyone on base made it but Sandy was running like a bullet to home. The player picked up the ball and threw it to home. Sandy jumped over the catcher and: BOOM! He landed on home plate and that was the best comeback ever because they won the game. That day I learned that determination is everything.

Maybe that's why it was the best game ever. The fans left happy.

Esteban Vazquez
Rafael Hernandez School

## Smarter

| S | M | A | R | T | E | R |
|---|---|---|---|---|---|---|
| *School is a kid's way to get smarter.* | *Math is my very best subject in school.* | *Algebra is the same thing as math.* | *Remember to get everything you need to be prepared for school.* | *Take music classes to become a musician.* | *Every time you take a test be prepared so you will be smarter.* | *Remember to participate in school activities.* |

Joseily Williams
Dr. E. Alma Flagg School

# Winter Weather

When I was ten years old I had the best winter ever. My cousin and I got to make snow angels. It was fun. I ate a lot of cakes that my cousins and I baked. One of the best cakes we made is called a Flan and it was so yummy.

My little sister and I watched cartoons sitting under covers. We both enjoyed the cartoons.

At first I thought that winter was going to be so cold and boring because of the snow. We wouldn't be able to go anywhere. But I learned that winter can be fun. We had lots of fun going to winter parties and going to slumber parties. Everyone was outside shoveling and playing in the snow. My cousin, Mathew, and I were sliding down the snow on sliding boards.

Then the winter weather started to get colder and colder every single day. But inside my house we stayed warm.

Darleen Hodge
Rafael Hernandez School

# Playing Basketball

When I was eight years old my aunt showed my how to play basketball. I was happy that Aunt Rasheeda showed me. I learned how to shoot and play one-on-one.

When I was 11 years old I played baseball and I did not like it. But I played it. I started getting good and I was on a team and the team was a good team. But they liked to fight when they lost and they got mad and sad. I told them not to be mad.

We stopped fighting and we got better. They listened to my advice and we played our game. I told them teamwork will make a good plan for winning our games. It did!

Kasson Morman
Bragaw Avenue School

## How I Got Smarter

This is a story of how I got smarter: animal-wise.
This is how it started...

"We're going to the zoo!  We're going to the zoo!" I said bouncing up and down in my seat as we were traveling to the Turtle Back Zoo for the first time.

"We're here! We're here!" I said as I ran out of the car to the front gate as my mom paid for our admission.

"Ohhh, what kind of animal is that?" I said with a lot of amazement.

"That's an Arctic fox and her cubs," the zoo ranger said.

"Wow, she's beautiful, so are her cubs. They're dazzling with beauty," I said with a lot of expression.

"That's why she's endangered," the zoo ranger told me.

"What's endangered?" I asked in a soft voice.

"Huh? Endangered is when a species is in danger of being extinct," the ranger said with a sad look in his eyes.

"Oh, that is sad, Ranger. That's why I want to become an animal saver to help animals that are endangered. That's what I want to be when I grow up!" I said with happiness.

Ever since that day at the zoo I have loved animals.

Saalih TaaHaa
Bragaw Avenue School

## Smarter, Smarter

I got smarter by learning my ABC's and 123's. Also, I got smarter by reading. My school has a special reading class that helps me read even more.

The subject I like best is math. I like math because I like fractions and numbers.

Eddaleez Santaliz
Dr. E. Alma Flagg School

## Smarter

If you're in school,
You don't have to be cool.
So, if you're smart
You could go to art.
When you're in class
It's like an hourglass.
Time flies by.
When you want to try,
Math games are fun,
So you don't have to run.
You can read and write all night.
The next day you might get the answers right.
It's like a plan
Not a hologram.
When you get to college
You'll have a lot of knowledge.

Ibrahima Toure
Miller Street Academy

## How Are You Smarter?

As we go around, people say that they are dumb and not smart; but that's when they are wrong. Everybody in the world is smart and they get smarter every day. We may be different but we all learn some things.

When we were born, our first teachers were our parents. They taught us what's right or wrong and how to do things. While the years went past, other people, such as teachers, came in the picture. And, like our parents, the teachers taught us even more. From being a baby to turning into a big girl or boy, we got smarter. Then, we learned even more helpful things such as math, science, language arts, social studies, and so much more.

In school, kids don't answer or ask questions. But then again, doing that helps you get smarter. Asking questions helps you understand the lesson. So, that way, if you take a test it is going to be a piece of cake.

Nana Musah
Miller Street Academy

# Don't Say Anything

There was once a lonely girl named Clarisse. She was 11 years old and in the sixth grade. She was always being teased and having her heart broken. The worst part was that she had no friends at school. She wished she had at least one friend, but all of them were the same—mean, grouchy, and disrespectful.

She was like an invisible girl who many believed should have been named: Ugly Old Hairy Clarisse. (That was the name that the cheerleaders called her behind her back). She had always been nice and friendly, but everyone treated her like trash and no one liked her.

She lived at 123 BarfUp Street. She also had some mean friends: DJ, Hood, Big Daddy, and Big Boss. She was so tired of them. She wished they would stop teasing her because it was making her life miserable. She hated it because they had bothered her since kindergarten.

When Clarisse went to her first day of school, she saw girls and boys all over the playground. She started to get nervous and sat on the benches, alone. Clarisse sat there and reached out for a book to read and waited until they called her name.

A moment later, they had finally called her to Room #324. She was anxious about going to class where no one had liked her last year and she hoped she had at least a friend—only one this year because everybody looked at her as if she were a bad person. She sat down and said, "Hi, how are you doing?" to everyone. Then they all noticed that she was a friendly girl after all and that her name was Clarisse. She had wanted some friends for a long time since she herself knew that she was a nice person to talk to. Having friends would be a plus, since she could tell all her secrets to someone.

Clarisse sat and the teacher introduced herself to the class and said, "Welcome everyone. My name is Mrs. Fun." Everyone had asked why her name was Mrs. Fun. She told them she was called Mrs. Fun because she had been fun to all her kids and everyone liked her as a teacher and a mom—especially her own kids—they loved her.

The teacher told them that she will have parties every Friday and on the students' birthdays. Everyone was surprised and happy to see what would happen next. She even had a treat for the ones who had been good for the day and on each day different students would have a prize. Clarisse felt like she would like this class even more and she would have the whole class as her friends because now everyone liked her.

The teacher had even had a welcome party for the new students who had come to her class. Later, her best friends were Cynthia and Clarabelle. Cynthia and Clarabelle had lots and lots of fun together and they told each other secrets and what they liked about each other. From then on Clarisse was so happy because she learned being nice to someone and being true to you is the best way to make good friends.

Julissa Zambrano (writing and drawing)
Rafael Hernandez School

**Stay in School**

Stay in school
Don't be a fool
Don't do drugs
You want to be smart
So don't you start
You will go to college
To get more knowledge
Set your goal high
So you will qualify
So stay in school
Remember not to be a fool

Yaa Sarpong
McKinley School

Amaryllis Mendez
McKinley School

## If You Don't Have Anything Good

Have you ever heard the expression, "If you don't have anything good to say, don't say anything at all?"  Well, I'm going to tell you a story about a person who did not follow this good advice.

There once was a boy who lived in Newark, New Jersey, in a little house. He was a mean jerk and picked on kids every day because they had everything he wanted. He was just a poor red headed 11-year-old boy named Danny who went to North Star. One day he was going to school. He saw that one of his classmates, Jerry, was telling people he got the newest game system. So, Danny walked up to him and said, "You need to take a shower, you smell like a wet dog."

He hit the game system out of Jerry's hand and started running. He ran to class because he was late. When our teacher, Ms. Mandy, asked why he was late he said, "My mother needed my help cleaning." So I went to take a seat and wrote a note to Timmy about what happened. He called him a green frog. He didn't say anything back. Timmy thinks he was just scared of Jerry. "RING, RING!!!"  The bell rang. It was time to go to lunch.

Danny didn't have any money so he went up to Manny and asked if he could have his food. He said, "NO!" So Danny said, "Fatso, you're always eating so give it to me." Danny turned around and the teacher was right there behind him watching. She was told by the other kids that Danny was picking on them and messing up their games. She wanted to go and see it for herself and she did.

Danny was sent to the Principal's office for a sit down talk. The school sent Danny to a school where kids learn how to treat people the right way. Danny went the same day. The school told his parents that he would be there for two days. During the time he was there, Timmy and Manny found out why he acted the way he did and why he acts the way he often acts. Danny was acting out because they had the things that Danny wanted and couldn't have. Danny didn't have the money to buy the nice things that his classmates had.

When Danny returned to school all the kids in his class said they were sorry about his situation but that his situation should not make him treat them differently. So, for the rest of the day, Danny said sorry to all the kids he had picked on and bullied. And he learned something that day, "If you don't have something nice to say, don't say anything at all."

Tanajah Jenkins
Rafael Hernandez School

# How Did I Get Smarter?

I got smarter by listening and being patient. When I was younger I loved playing soccer. I was so good that my dad signed me up to be part of a team. I was excellent but the coach thought I wasn't so good. I eventually found out the problem was how I acted. I never listened to the coach. When he said: "Pass the ball" I got impatient and got mad. I didn't make the team. I came back the next year less aggravated and more cooperative with teammates. I made the team that year.

I've learned soccer isn't just about kicking soccer balls but about being patient, listening more, and working with others. Soccer helped me become a smarter person. You could probably learn something too from my story.

Nenseh Koneh
Dr E. Alma Flagg School

# Good Advice

There was a boy named Joey. He would push people or throw food on them everyday in the lunchroom. Often times, people would cry or simply feel terrible. Joey would never say, "I'm sorry."

Joey also had a funny voice. He spoke with a foreign accent. He claimed he was from France. That's why he talked with a French accent. (He had to stop playing tricks on everyone because he was bound to get suspended for being such a bully).

Joey didn't care about the consequences of his actions until one day a new kid came to school. His name was Robert. Joey started *hiking on* Robert right away. He started saying things like, "Hey, nice shoes. Where do you shop, Payless?" All of a sudden Robert came back at him and said, "What do you care, Frenchy." Joey was shocked. "What did you just call me?" Robert repeated, "Frenchy!"

No one had ever had the nerve to tell Joey off but Robert did. After that, other people started standing up for themselves and making fun of Joey! (Not to be mean but to teach him a lesson).

Joey had never been more embarrassed in his life. He decided to start being nice to people. So he learned his lesson. "If you don't have anything nice to say, don't say anything at all."

Corey Guthrie
Rafael Hernandez School

## Better at Cooking

At a very early age I felt I wasn't really *special*. I thought that I should find something that I loved, so I searched. By the time I was six I woke up and smelled something really good, and went to see what it was. When I went to see what it was I happened to see eggs, bacon, and toast on the kitchen table. In my mind I said, "Hmmm, maybe I should learn how to cook." Then I started to watch my mom cook everyday until I got tired of watching my mother cook and wanted to start doing.

I was seven when I cooked my first meal. It wasn't the best experience but it was the best attempt. I made corn and string beans with mashed potatoes but apparently almost burned my house down. That's when I fanned my smoke detector, and everything was okay after I was done. Maybe I still needed to step back, watch, and learn.

I began to watch my mother cook again until I was nine. Then gave it another try and my food was so wonderful! I was so proud of myself and my mom was too. Now she wants me to cook for her from now on!

Hynasia Cromer
Bragaw Avenue School

## The Sleepover

Have you ever heard the expression, "What goes around comes around?" Well, you are about to read a story of the time that saying came to life.

One year, on my birthday, Niesha had given me a gift. It was a phone. It felt like it was as smooth as a new poster.

Months later, on Niesha's birthday, I traveled to her house without a gift. When we got to Niesha's house I had forgotten her birthday gift. So I needed to do something.

I decided to go to the store and get her a gift. I was going to pay for the gift with money I had earned from babysitting. I decided to get her a gift because I wanted her to feel as special as she made me feel when she gave me a gift. I tried to find something that she would appreciate.

Even though gifts are not as important as the thought behind the act, I learned that, "What goes around come around," because when you do something nice for someone, they might do something nice back for you.

Julia Green
Rafael Hernandez School

## I Am

I'm fabulous

Talkative

Strong

Kind

I love math and I also love books.

I love playing basketball.

I like monkeys because they are so friendly.

I rather come to school than stay at home.

I am Aliyah Sweeney

Aliyah Sweeney
Newton Street School


## Smart

Some students are very talented.
Most of my friends always make smart decisions...(sometimes).
Are you smart and talented?
Ready to help other children make smart decisions as well?
Today the world has smart people in it
Because
People like you help people be smart.

Jada Nesbitt
Newton Street School


## How Did I Get Smarter?

I got smarter in basketball by doing what I was supposed to be doing. Sometimes I play point guard, sometimes I play shooting guard.

When I first used to play basketball I was not very good but when I practiced more and more I got very good at it.

Brandon Mendez
Dr E. Alma Flagg School

## Bad Girls

Have you ever heard the saying, "Don't judge a book by its cover?" Well, you are about to read a story of two bad girls on the playground that thought that they owned the place.

These two girls were named Kelly and Julia. Kelly was tall and Julia was talkative.

One day they had mean faces. I went outside and said to myself, "What am I getting myself into?" But I went to talk to them anyway. I said, "Can you please try to not be so mean?"

They may have been surprised that I asked them to stop being mean. Maybe what I asked made them think about their actions. Whatever it was, they started to make an effort to change.

Kelly and Julia taught me to never judge a book by its cover because you wouldn't like to be judged. Julia and Kelly learned that it was a bad mistake to be mean and not to judge people either.

Alea Williams
Rafael Hernandez School

## Smarter

Being smart
Will lead you on your way
Being smart
I will say
Will get you good grades
Will make you proud
Be smart!

Zakeeyiah Sellars
McKinley School

## Smarter

I can get smarter by studying and by writing each word on a sheet of paper 10 times each. I have to do extra work too.

I love school. I don't like to stay home because there is nothing to do there but play the video game and watch TV.

Earl McFarland
Dr. William H. Horton School

# KNOWLEDGE

**K**    Keeping on task

**N**    No nonsense

**O**     Outstanding performances

**W**    Willing to learn

**L**    Learning everything you can

**E**    Educating myself as much as possible

**D**    Determined to learn

**G**    Getting to know my work better

**E**    Everlasting knowledge

Tia Cotton
Dr. E. Alma Flagg School

## The Woods

Julia and I had a project to complete for our class. Our scheduled camping trip was perfect timing! We would use that time to find the rocks we needed to complete our projects. We had no idea that finding rocks in the woods would make us get lost.

While Julia and I were in the woods camping, we picked out some rocks for our project at school. We started to walk around; finding more rocks in the woods. As the sun started to go down, we started looking inside our book bags for our flashlights. The flashlights did not have batteries and it was getting darker and I was getting scared. Julia used her experience with camping to make a fire.

Next time I will bring batteries for my flashlight. But if I forget I will know how to make the best of the situation by making a fire.

Niesha Reece
Rafael Hernandez School

# The New Puppet

"Never give up." This story is about two friends, a puppet, and Layla's puppy named Pal.

Layla and Jake went to the store to buy a puppet. The puppet was $3.96. Layla paid $10.96; she had $7.00 left. Pal really loved the puppet so Layla let him have it.

Layla figured that since she and Jake lived next door to each other, they could share the puppet. Later that same day, they went to the candy store. No dogs were allowed in the store so Pal stayed outside. The friends paid $2.81 for three candy bars—one for Layla, one for Jake and one for Pal. They now had $4.19 left.

When they came out of the candy store, Pal was gone. "Where is he?" asked Jake. "I thought I put him on the leash," Layla said. They decided to buy some supplies for Pal. The supplies came to $4.19, the last of the money.

They started to look for Pal. "Pal, where are you?" Jake said in a soft voice. "Pal, we've got chocolate," said Layla. "Pal, where are you? Pal, we miss you." Layla and Jake said in a sad voice. Finally they started to pack up. "Pal," Layla said. They started to give up. "Let's go home," Jake said.

When they got home they saw Pal. "Pal," Layla said in a loud voice. "The puppet and Pal have been in the house for three hours," said father. Everyone was happy and they all hugged each other.

I learned that you should never give up. Just when you think you've lost, you end up winning in the end.

Jaquan Williams
Rafael Hernandez School

# How I Got Smarter

My name is Coran, and I am going to tell you how I got smarter.

I got smarter by first going to school and getting my education. My favorite subject is math. I like math because I like learning the multiples of numbers.

Have you ever heard of special reading programs? If you have, aren't they fun? They help you with reading, spelling, and words. When I was little, I used to learn my ABC's and 123's. But now I am in the sixth grade, and now I learn much more.

I hope you take my advice and learn how to get smarter.

Coran Kelly
Dr. E. Alma Flagg School

Israel Alford, Miller Street School

**Smarter**

What does it mean to become smarter?
**brain + studying + learning + listening to the teacher.**
You can get smarter by studying, learning, and listening to your teacher.

Sade Narvaez
Dr. E. Alma Flagg School

Maria Heredia, McKinley School

## Smarter

**S**mart is not a delusion in your mind

**M**ind is heart to grades

**A**ny brain muscle will lead you to becoming smarter

**R**ead to expand your knowledge for life

**T**eachers teach you to be smart for school

**E**veryone is happy when their brain's smart

**R**emember: Be smart for your own sake!

Mike Beato
McKinley School

## Being Thankful For Learning Strong Values

I am thankful for the values that my family has taught me. I have grown wiser because of them and their teaching. I am thankful for my family. My family includes my father, mother, and big brother.

Why am I thankful? I'm thankful for my family because my family loves me. They want me to do well in school and not to do any bad things. My loving family always wants me to be a happy and successful boy. Those are reasons I'm thankful for my beautiful family. I learned from them to be a generous boy and to be kind to others. They helped me to learn how to overcome hard times and find peace.

How has my family influenced me? A way that they influence me is that they help me become a better person. I treat all my friends with respect. I have manners that my parents have taught me and try to pass it on to others. This is why I'm thankful in all things.

Daniel Marin
Ridge Street School

## Crash

"Wow, this red car is about to hit us," Dan thought to himself. Dan turned around and told his father. The car was going an excessive speed. It was red and it was going to hit us. Moments before they crashed, Dan's father said, "I don't know what you are talking about Dan." Dan asked his father to look in the mirror.

"Oh no!" Then the car crashed…boom!!! The engine broke down. Everyone seemed to be okay—they didn't get hurt too badly. Dan's arm was injured but he was okay. The tow truck came. The tow truck took Dan and his dad the rest of the way to Baltimore. They thanked the tow truck driver for helping them out. The guy in the red car who caused the crash went to jail.

While in Baltimore, Dan's dad bought a new car. It was a big, silver Mercedes Benz. When they got back home Dan told his mother he had a great time in Baltimore. He was very tired by then so he went to sleep.

Dan loved his father but believed that his father should have listened to him in the first place. He thought about the possible outcomes and realized an important lesson: Just because something happens doesn't mean it has to stop you from reaching your goal.

Jose Figueroa
Dr. William H. Horton School

# SMART MATH

**S**     Subtracting, Simplifying, Surrounding, Shapes,

**M**    Multiplication,

**A**    Adding, Algebra,

**R**    Radius, Rational, Rectangles,

**T**    Triangles, Timetables,

**M**    Multiples, Measurements,

**A**    Algebraic Numbers,

**T**    Translations,

**H**    Hexagon, Hemisphere,

Yanializ Alicea
Hawkins Street School

Joshua Paredes, Miller Street School

## Smart So Far

How I got to be this smart at this point was not as easy as you may think. It took a lot of practice to get where I am. Before I went to kindergarten my mother made me write my name and letters of the alphabet five times each. After I started doing that it was kind of fun but after a while it was a little boring.

Because of all the work I did, I'm now in the sixth grade with great teachers. I thank all the people who got me here and I thank myself for letting myself make it here. I have a long way to go but I will be a success because I am smart.

Shakira Major
Dr. E. Alma Flagg School

### *Some Day*

*Some day I wish to be a stepper*

*Hurry up, some day!*

*At home I practice*

*To become a smarter stepper*

*Nothing to do but step*

*Day by day I practice*

*Each day I am one day closer to*

*Entering a stepping contest*

Sharonda Byrd
Bragaw Avenue School

## How I Got Smarter

The way I got smarter is by paying attention and doing class work. Preschool was all about nap time, playing and drawing. In kindergarten it was writing your name and learning your manners. First grade was all about math and literacy. In second grade it was about reviewing things and learning new things. Third through fifth grade was all about the NJ Ask Test. The teachers got you whatever help you needed because they wanted you to graduate to the next grade.

I don't know what sixth grade is like because I just started but I think it is easy and hard at some points. But sometimes it can be too much. This is how I've gotten smarter!!!!!!!!!

Mikayla Wideman
Dr. E. Alma Flagg School

# I Got Smarter

I got smarter playing soccer because at practice my coach always told me that I should make up a strategy to keep the ball away from my opponent. My coach also told me to keep a sharp eye on my opponent's speed, movement, and strategy.

After a few tries I finally got the hang of it. That is how I got smarter in playing soccer.

Erick Berrocal
Dr. E. Alma Flagg School

# SMARTER

Successful socially and mentally

Able to just run through
Everything like it is nothing.

Becoming smarter isn't about cramming everything into your head.

It is about making choices in life and being able to say "yes" and "no" when you need to.

Kaomi Burgos
Dr. E. Alma Flagg School

# Smarter

I got smarter because I am in a special reading program. It helps you with spelling and reading words. Because of this program I can read better than before.

My mother and my teachers influence me to work hard. I go to Mrs. Shilling-Ford for math and she helps me with math. I've been with her for two years. If she didn't push me hard in the fifth grade I would not have passed math.

This is how I got smarter.

Rosetta Wolo
Dr. E. Alma Flagg School

**How to Be Smart on a Fresh Start**

We came a long way from there
Until today
Learning is like an art
That comes from the heart

That's why we're so smart

We fought and we ran
We played hide and go seek
Until we came up

Young women and young men,

We must be adroit with our work
Keep working hard
It won't hurt
We are successful at dreaming
That's why we keep achieving
Because we keep believing

When you believe
You achieve
When you proceed
You will not grieve
This is how you level up
To college
To learn better knowledge

To get your degree
You have to get A's and B's
That's how to stay smart
On a fresh start!

Aliyah Coleman
McKinley School

# How I Got Smarter

Hello, my name is Destinee. I am going to tell you how I got smarter.

I got smarter by listening in class. Also, I got smarter by getting good grades. Getting smarter is important to me because when I go to high school I will think everything is easy. I am also good in math. Math is great. Without math you will not get a job.

I am in the sixth grade and I am surprised I made it to the sixth grade. I will graduate from college and be able to see Mrs. Bailey and Mrs. Larwa if they have not retired.

Destinee Odom
Dr. E. Alma Flagg School

Brianna
Angueira

Miller
Street
School

# How Did I Get Smarter?

The way I got smarter is by studying, practicing, and most importantly paying attention in class. One of the problems I had in class was talking a lot with my friends. I got in trouble and I learned a lesson. I don't talk anymore unless my teacher says it's okay.

I learn new words. In science I learn about the microscope and I know the parts of a microscope because I talk less in class.

That is how I got smarter.

Alexis Reyes
Dr. E. Alma Flagg School

# Classroom Work

What does it mean to become "smarter?" How did you get "smarter?"

The way you get smarter is finishing school, which means completing middle school, high school, and college to get a degree.

I am in middle school and it is a lot of fun in science because we do experiments. But my favorite subject is math.

How do you get good grades?

I get good grades by passing my tests and doing homework. Homework is just like school work but it is only called homework.

I am smart because I listen to my parents and I respect other people but first I have to respect myself.

Genesis Martinez
Dr. E. Alma Flagg School

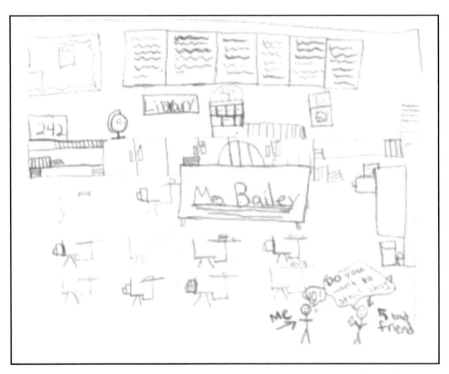

Adrian Torres
Dr. E. Alma Flagg School

## Smarter in Baseball

I am smarter in baseball. You have to think smarter in the field. For example, when the ball is hit to the infield and it is coming towards you, you have to think smart and throw the ball to first base and get the runner out.

If a runner is on first base and the ball is hit to second base you can go for a double play.

Now let's talk about batting. If you get on base, you have to look at the coach and he may tell you to steal a base.

Baseball is not just about hitting and running. Players must be smart in making plays. Baseball is not for dummies.

Robert Carrasco
Dr. E. Alma Flagg School


## Thank You Means Smarter

I am thankful for many things like family and health. Being thankful is a part of being smarter. I'm mainly thankful for being in school with my wonderful teachers and friends because they help me be smarter. I'm thankful for my friends because without them I probably wouldn't have many friends at Ridge Street. I wouldn't have anyone to tell jokes to. I wouldn't have my friends Osayre, Karina, and Sariah. I wouldn't be able to hear their laughter every morning. I can never have enough friends and I can never thank mine enough.

I'm also thankful for my teachers because without them I wouldn't have an education. Without my teachers from K-6, I wouldn't have an education. In the old days, some people didn't get to finish school and to get an education and some never even went to school. However, I have the opportunity with the help of amazing teachers. The teachers I have now in sixth grade are a pleasure and I thank each and every one of them.

In closing, I would like to say I'm thankful for my friends, teachers, and family. I've learned two things. First, you can't have enough friends or even enough education. Next, I've learned you should give thanks for everything once in a while.

Ibreyanah Turner
Ridge Street School

## School

It's somewhere that I go
Monday through Friday
Not to chill in the hall
That's **not** how
I spend my day
But to learn

I stay in class from eight to three
And at lunch
I like to read my favorite book
By my favorite tree

My objective is
To get a degree in writing
So that I can become an author
But don't forget math
I love math
It's my favorite subject in school

I am a math whiz
It's fun and really cool
I wish I could stay in school 24/7
But I must go home
To do the worst part of school:

***THE HOMEWORK!!***

Lizetta Roselli
McKinley School

## How I Became Smarter

When I was four years old, I went to a daycare and they taught me math, science and how to write. When I turned five, I was transferred to Dr. E. Alma Flagg School because I was old enough to go to a real school and meet new friends.

When I got to school, I did not know anyone. So, it felt weird. After I got comfortable, I knew I was going to like Dr. E. Alma Flagg, and I did.

By second grade I learned the numbers, alphabets, and the months of the year. I also met a friend from Peru named Erick and we've been friends for the past four years. When I got to the sixth grade I thought about all the things I've been taught. For example, I've learned how to use lattice and about novels. I miss Kindergarten through fifth grades. Without the school work that I've done in the past I would not be able to do the school work I'm doing in the present.

This is how I became smarter.

Kawuan Hordge
Dr. E. Alma Flagg School

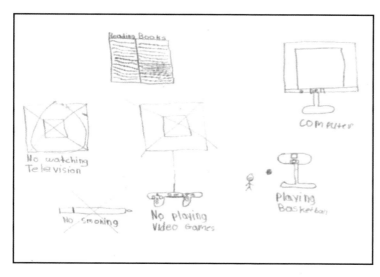

Maurice Rogers

Dr. E. Alma Flagg School

## What Does Smarter Mean?

Everybody thinks smarter means to go to school and to do your homework. Also, to do well in the following subjects: math, language arts, science, and social studies and go to college. I used to think that too. But what I think smart really means is to make your own decisions; to follow your dreams and do what's right. That's smart.

Tatiyana Sabb
Dr. E. Alma Flagg School

**Dreaming of Acting**

Acting and dreaming
Aren't they the same thing?
Life
Believing is all about mingling.
Achieving
Mingling around, singing with sound.
No, it's me who shall take the acting crown.

Marlaine Erisnord
Bragaw Avenue School

Steven Herrera
Miller Street School

## Basketball

I was a boy with no basketball skills. But now I got more game than most people I know. The way I got my game up is by practicing 24/7. I started playing with teams that weren't any good. Now, I play for "Battle of the Bricks" and "AAU" and "Future Generation of Leaders." My father, uncle, and cousins helped me get my game up. Now, I can shoot a ball from full court and make it. I also can dunk in 8-feet baskets and higher. I can even play better than some of my friends and cousins. I am almost the best I can be. I am looking forward to going to the NBA.

Now people call "Hazy" the best in ball. I am almost better than Kobe. I know I am the best you have ever seen.

Haamid Abdullah
Bragaw Avenue School

## Go to School

Being smarter
Is helpful with everyday life
Be smart and become a better person
It will lead you to college
Being smarter
Can get you a good career

Zahire Hannah and Nicodemo Rivera
McKinley School

## Basketball

I made my first shot in a real hoop at the age of four. I did this by observing family members and friends shoot and line up themselves so that the hoop would be equal with their shoulders.

When I was on a basketball team, the first thing my coach said was in order to be on the team you have to know all the positions. I learned that you have to be patient so that the coach can know that your attitude is good. The coach was on me because he knew I was good and my attitude was good. He wanted me to be better.

Elijah Lott
Bragaw Avenue School

# Family Times

"Gobble, Gobble!" my brother said as I walked across the hall. It was our annual Thanksgiving family dinner and we were all excited, all for me. I just wanted to watch the new special movie that was airing today. Too bad my mom disagrees with me. She just wants my siblings and me to spend time with my family. How selfish!

Well now I'm at the table. They're serving turkey, rice, beans, and pumpkin pie. I just have to rush through this since the movie starts at 7:00. If I can sneak to the room AND close the door, AND turn off the light, I might have a chance. Gulllpp! Whew, done with dinner. Now Amanda should be waiting for me at the first post.

"So the whole thing is pretty self explanatory. All you have to do is crawl through the vent and meet Julian on the other side," Amanda said. I think she had to distract mom because I almost blew the whole mission when I screamed at the top of my lungs, "Spider!"

As I reached the end, I saw my brother outside. "Just use this rope and grappling hook to reach your window then climb," he said.

This would have been easy only my dad walked in while I was climbing through the window and busted me for not spending time with the family. A wiser me has realized that I was the selfish one.

Joshua DeJesus
Ridge Street School

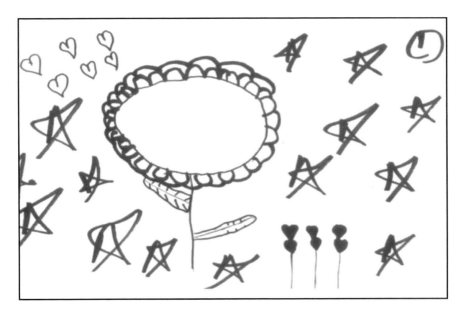

Tanaya Williams
Chancellor Avenue School

## Cooking

The thing that I always wanted to get smart at is cooking. I love to cook, but I just don't know how to cook. I always get help from my stepmother and my father.

I like to cook a lot of things, especially rice, beans, and chicken. The problem is that I never knew the recipe for them, but I still like to cook them. I really wish I had the recipes for all the foods I like to cook. I never thought to try out my own recipes. I didn't think that I was ever going to get it right. I was always telling myself, "I cannot cook at all."

Then one day I took a chance. I cooked every day until I got it right. I knew that I could do it. I always trusted myself. I love cooking and if you try it I know that you will love it too. Cooking is really fun.

After I could cook all by myself I felt really excited. I thought that day was the best day of my life. Anyone would feel that way when they keep trying and never give up. They would really feel happy about themselves.

One of the reasons why I learned how to cook is because I never gave up. I know that you can do it too. Every time you do something and you are not good at it yet, keep practicing, studying, and trying and never give up.

Tania Pujois
Bragaw Avenue School

## Singing

Singing is a hard thing to do. One day I was trying to sing and broke my mother's favorite glass. That let me know that I could not sing. If were going to sing, I would have to learn how.

It was hard for me to learn how to sing. But that didn't stop me from practicing and practicing. By the time I finished practicing at home my mother decided to send me off to singing class.

My singing teacher, Mrs. Hibbard, helped me with all of my singing problems. Mrs. Hibbard taught me all I needed to know. When I got home I started singing perfectly.

I felt so proud of myself. I have achieved what not many people could have. Becoming smarter is one of the greatest things you can do.

Delores Tarry
Bragaw Avenue School

**Smarter**

Smarter is the feeling to be,
More intelligent than the people you see.
To do this you must always obey
Your teacher, each and every day
You must also know that not each day
Is made for you to run and play.
There are times for you to learn,
So your passion for your subjects burn
To become smarter you must train your mind,
And you will be surprised at the thing you will find.

Victor Dike
Bragaw Avenue School

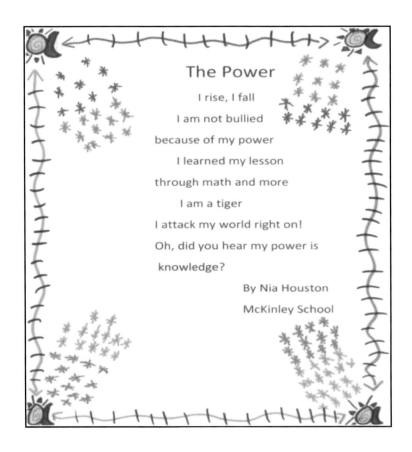

The Power

I rise, I fall
I am not bullied
because of my power
I learned my lesson
through math and more
I am a tiger
I attack my world right on!
Oh, did you hear my power is
knowledge?

By Nia Houston
McKinley School

## Anything

I float, I sting
I can be anything
I can be this
I can be that
I can be the president
If I want to do that
That's what I mean
When I want to be anything
That's my dream
To be anything,
To do, to be
Anything.

Mathew Nelson
Bragaw Avenue School

## How I Got Smarter

When I was in fifth grade I had a problem. My problem was that I got a C in gym. I always had all A's. I improved my C by packing an extra pair of sneakers and sweats in my book bag. My grade went from a C to a B then to an A+.

I said to myself, "my report card is complete and so was my gym grade." I accomplished my goal to improve my grade again!!

Uniqua Collins
Bragaw Avenue School

**Smart**

**S**chool is cool.
**M**s. Notar has a very good class.
**A**rt is like painting.
**R**unning is important.
**T**hinking questions.

Jose Cruz
Hawkins Street School

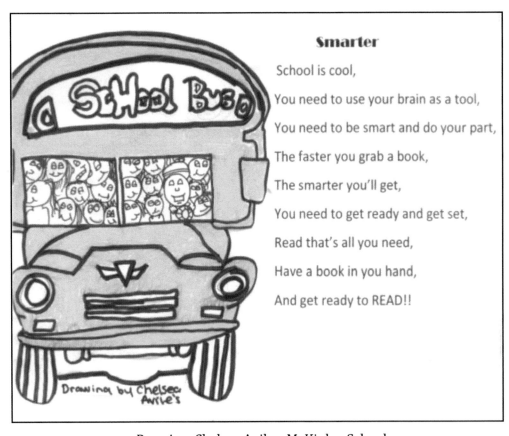

**Smarter**

School is cool,

You need to use your brain as a tool,

You need to be smart and do your part,

The faster you grab a book,

The smarter you'll get,

You need to get ready and get set,

Read that's all you need,

Have a book in you hand,

And get ready to READ!!

Drawing by Chelsea Aviles

Drawing: Chelsea Aviles, McKinley School
Poem: Keyshalee Matos, McKinley School

## Obama Smarter Report

Obama made a speech at a high school in September 2009. He talked about goals. He talked about studying instead of spending all of our time playing games. He did it so students can be responsible for their education.

My most favorite part of Obama's speech was when he said that we shouldn't spend every day playing games so we can study. That is how I feel. I think the most important part is when he talked about other people's successes. It showed me that there is no excuse for not doing your work!

Edwin Arroyo
McKinley School

## I Am Thankful For My Scar

I am most thankful for the scar on my left pointer finger. It all started when I was just a little girl. I thought that a piece of glass that was on the floor was a toy. My grandmother placed me on the kitchen floor and accidentally stepped on my hand. My finger went into the glass and I began to bleed. She patched me up herself, but I wouldn't call this the best experience. I can surely tell you that now it's worth it because it's my one memory of her.

As a kid I probably thought that this was the worst thing that could have happened to me. Now I actually notice that this had a good purpose. It's not really as bad as it sounds. There is always a lesson to learn no matter the circumstance. For instance, from this I learned that some memories can come from a situation that we think is bad in the moment. In other words, memories can change some bad situations into good ones, like what happened to me.

What happened to me has taught me that even though I went through physical pain, now every time I look at my finger I have an everlasting memory of my grandmother. The scar is there for life and I want to remember her forever also. With what happened to me with my scar, I see how when you love someone all things have a connection with them. This influenced me to give my family members things so that they can have a remembrance of me. For example, I can give them a postcard, earrings, and any small object that has a significant connection between us.

I truly do not know if you have a memory of someone special, but I will tell you to give someone or get a memory prior to you regretting it. You can even make a memory by doing something that you normally wouldn't do. Memories are natural to life, so if you don't have one, MAKE ONE!

Nicole Pimentel
Ridge Street School

# What I Did To Become Smarter

I became smarter in a peculiar way. My story began in the year 1999. My mother wanted to work, so she thought it was best for my brother and me to go to our native country on the continent of Africa, her native land. She also thought it would help us speak her language. I was two and my brother was nine months old. By September 18, 1999 we were on an airplane with our mother. We reached the continent of Africa and lived there for four years.

By the time we came back, I was six years old and my brother was four. It was bone chilling cold when we came back on January 4, 2003. I couldn't speak English and neither could my brother. I could write my ABC's and say my two time tables. Without a doubt, it was hard. Really hard. So, when we came my mother tried to test us. She gave me a pen and paper and did the same with my brother.

My brother sat dumbfounded and stared at me. I wrote my ABC's and caught my mother's attention. Then she told me to write simple words. That is when it was my turn to be dumbfounded. I couldn't do it. Nothing, absolutely nothing of that matter made sense to me. That's when my mother knew it was time to work. *Work hard.*

We were homeschooled for two years. We got up at 8:00am and started "classes" at 8:30am. We worked from 8:30am to 11:00pm. No TV. Seven days. We studied hard! There were times when my mother got frustrated but she never gave up.

Reading use to be my worst subject. I couldn't read or speak English. So, I hated it. I started regular school in the fall of 2004. I was set to sit near a girl named J. Unlike the other kids, J. never laughed at me or made fun of me. She was always there when I couldn't understand something in class. Thanks to my mother I love reading and enjoy it very much.

I owe a big thank you to my mother. It brings me to tears whenever I think about it.

So, this is how I became smarter: by God's grace and my mother's helping hand. She may not be rich or famous, but she has a heart and love big enough for all the kids in the world.

How many Hollywood stars can say that?

Queenstar-Annane Banini
McKinley School

## My Life

Yo! Yo! Check it
Be all you can be
You can be the greatest like Muhammad Ali
Don't patronize me
Check it!

Knowledge is power
I know what I know
The more I learn
The farther I can go

In life, I know I can do this
Rain on my head is like a big bliss
Do you know what I mean?
Like things come in my brain
And when I go to sleep, it comes out like rain.

So I'm getting smart
In my body, I have a bit of heart.
No one else knows
Until you let it show.

Elijah Shuler, Jr.
Miller Street Academy

## Smart

Everyone is smart.
You just need to follow your heart,
So you can turn smart.
Learn everyday
So you know what to say.
You can turn into a geek some day
It doesn't matter what people say.
If you can believe it,
You can achieve it.
Someday your teacher will be surprised,
Of what you have under your sleeve
So then she will know that you can achieve.

Christalie Gonzalez
Miller Street Academy

# Influences in My Life

I am thankful for my family, my teachers, and my friends. If it were not for these three important influences in my life, I wouldn't be the person I am today. These specific things inspire me to keep going.

I am thankful for my family because they encourage and support me. If they didn't support me I wouldn't be confident in myself. I don't think I would have accomplished many things if they didn't believe in me. When I was student of the month for September, my parents were really proud of me and showed it to me by taking me out to eat. Also, they show me support by giving me physical contact. When I do a good job in school they kiss me or hug me to show that material things are not the best reward. Sometimes I need to be encouraged with words that continue to give me motivation to do my best. This has taught me that I need my family to do good academically and spiritually. They influence me by teaching me discipline. They teach me to show respect and say "thank you" or "please."

If my teachers didn't have an influence on me then I probably wouldn't know the stuff I know. I am grateful that I have teachers that care for us, as students, and want us to succeed. For example, today my math teacher taught me that graphs are one of the easiest ways to solve a problem. This has taught me that I need teachers in my life. They influence me by teaching me right from wrong and bringing out the best in me academically. The other day Mrs. Clement was telling my class and me a story about how she made a big mistake. After the story, she advised us not to make the same bad choice she did.

I am thankful for my friends because they are the ones who encourage me to go to school and I have positive peer pressure from them. Since they do such a good job in school and know how to act, I hang out with them because they have a better impact on my life than someone who does poorly in school and doesn't care about themselves. This has taught me that I need friends who have the same interest in education as I do. They influence me by going to school, doing their work, and not caring about what others think of them.

If it were not for these three important things I wouldn't be the person I am today.

*Who or what influences you?*

Kaitlyn Comesanas
Ridge Street School

# My Life is a Gift

My life is a gift. I am able to share with my family, have special friends, travel to different states and countries, and do things that can help change the world for the better.

I'm thankful to be alive because of every day that I spend with my family. My family is very important to me. We do many things together. We share stories, watch TV, eat together and go many different places. Even when my father is far away from me, I am happy that I can see him on holidays and summer vacations. It is nice to have a life where people like my family care about me so very much.

I love to make friends every time I have a chance. I do many things with my friends in school and after. I'm glad that I can count on such special friends. We can pretend, we sometimes help each other with our homework, and I have a lot of fun when we do sleepovers. It is so much fun to be alive and to share and do many things with friends.

Another reason I'm thankful to be alive is because I can travel and know different states and countries. My family takes me around on road trips and on airplanes to visit new places and to see my relatives. Last summer we went to the Dominican Republic and almost every year we go to Puerto Rico and we will go to new places later on too. It is also nice to know about the United States. When we go on road trips we pass by many states and I love it.

The last reason why I'm thankful for my life is because I can help the world in different ways to make it better. One day in the future, I'm going to graduate from high school and then go to college. I really want to go to Georgia Tech and study for things that can make me smarter and that can help me do things in the world. Right now I can help the world when I recycle in my house and by making sure that I don't throw garbage around to keep this world green. I want to grow and help others such as homeless people and people that are less fortunate and have fewer things than me.

My life is very important because if I don't live a quality life, I will make my family sad. I want to help people and have fun with my family and friends. These are reasons why I'm very thankful for my life.

Andrew Morell
Ridge Street School

# Friends Are Important

I appreciate my friends because they always put a smile on my face when I'm feeling gloomy. In addition, they teach me valuable lessons that I will remember for the rest of my life.

One of my favorite lessons that a great friend taught me is that "if at first you don't succeed try, try again." This lesson has helped in so many ways. For instance, on my social studies test I received a C. I was devastated but my friend told me not to give up and to try again. I did as she said and I studied for my next social studies quiz. I was immediately pleased when I received my grade because I got an A. I am very thankful that my friend shared that saying with me because it encouraged me to keep on trying.

This lesson will certainly influence my life. In high school and college when I am struggling with my grades I will always think of the saying, "if at first you don't succeed try, try again," and it will give me the strength to give more effort to what I'm having challenges in. Not to mention, when I am looking for a job I will refer to this saying. If I don't get the job I won't moan and complain about it, I'll just keep on searching for another one. Do you think this lesson will help you as much as it has helped me?

In conclusion, I would like to thank all of my friends for everything they have done for me. But I would like to give a special thank you to my friend who shared this valuable lesson with me. It will encourage me to follow my dreams without giving up. I really hope you remember this lesson when things don't go your way, if you do, you can accomplish anything you set your mind to.

Sariah Gonzalez
Ridge Street School

**Smart Math**

**S**   Subtraction, sub, solution, shape, share equally,
**M**   Multiplication, millions place, math,
**A**   Add, addition, algebra,
**R**   Rounding, ruler,
**T**   Time tables, tape measure, time,

**M**   Multiples, measurement, measure,
**A**   Abundant numbers,
**T**   Tenths place, tens, thousands,
**H**   Hundreds place, hundreds,

Nicole Caetano
Hawkins Street School

Kevin Mizhquin
Dr. E. Alma Flagg School

**Smart Math**

**S**   Subtraction, solution,
**M**   Multiples,
**A**   Adding, angles,
**R**   Rounding numbers,
**T**   Triangles,

**M**   Multiplication facts,
**A**   Abundant numbers,
**T**   Tenths place, tens, thousands,
**H**   Hundreds place, hexagons,

Kierra Martin
Hawkins Street School

**Reading is the Key**

Reading is the key
To a better future
Books are good
For you
And for me

They make you smart
And help you read
Without books
We cannot be
It's the key
To being in the lead
Remember to always read

Reading is awesome
Just make it
Your special blossom

How far can books take you?
Here we are
Learning not to fight

Books are rich
Richer than gold
Don't ever forget to read

Reading can take you far away
So,
Take the chance to become someone
And make sure your future is bright

Reading is the path
Reading is fun
Almost like learning a ton
If you want to explore
Then get on the fun reading bus

You should read twice a day
Or maybe even four
Just remember
If you want to become someone
Then take the fun reading path.

Dionicia Hernandez
(poem and illustration)
McKinley School

Danny Torres
Rafael Hernandez School


## How Beautiful Is It

How beautiful is it when family
Shares autumns together!
Autumn holds special events when people dance and enjoy...
I love it when my family gathers together and shares so many things,
For example,
Love...
...the love that grows bigger and bigger between friends and family
... Smarter.

Darling Diaz
Rafael Hernandez School

## Change Gathers Family

I love
When the leaves change
Colors
Smart Colors

Helping the people to gather
The leaves, fun

It is cold
Very windy
I enjoy having fun with my family

Ingrid Calderon
Rafael Hernandez School

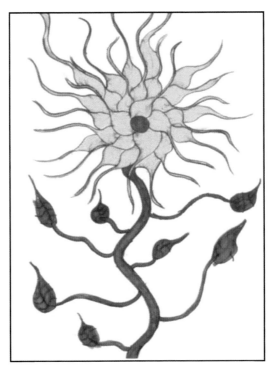

Derrick Wiltshire
Chancellor Avenue School

# Smarter: Grade 7 Contributors

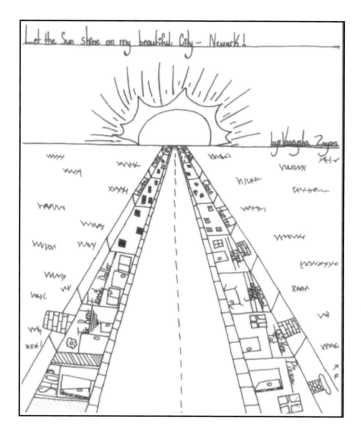

Vaneysha Zayaz, McKinley School

# Smarter

"Motivated" and "willingness" were the first words that infiltrated into my brain like an Apollo 13 launching into space when someone asked me "What does it mean to you to become smarter?" To me, to become smarter means to be successful and to be intelligent, going to high school and college, and becoming something big or important. I'd like to become a baseball player one day and run a program called *Achieve Your Dreams.* I would like to grow young kids' confidence up and would like to teach them that if you do well in school and believe in yourself, anything is possible. That's why I always try my very best in school and never give up.

This reminds me of the quote, "Education is the way to success that unlocks all doors." My interpretation of this quote implies that if you don't have an education you will never get anywhere in life or won't have a good job and will be stuck forever.

To me, to be smarter is a privilege because other students don't have the opportunity to listen to their teacher or get feedback from their teacher because the teacher may not care about the students' education like my smart and caring teacher Mr. Lichten. Other people just like to read from textbooks and like to copy work and get an A for that.

What I have done to become smarter is that I have been listening to my teachers. At first, every time Mr. Lichten would call on me I would nervously and anxiously answer. I always listen to Mr. Lichten because he is the best teacher you could ever have and I will probably never have another teacher like him. When my teacher teaches a subject he makes sure he teaches the same subject in a multitude of ways and gives examples so that we understand. My teacher, Mr. Lichten, is the reason why I am going to be smart. As my teacher is teaching me and my class writing, I am thinking to myself, "Wow, I can't believe that he is going to teach us the skills that we need to pass the state test."

I am smarter because I always listen to all of my teachers. I am smarter because I am open for feedback and I am dedicated to school. To be dedicated means to go to school and put 100% effort into all your work and when your teacher gives you feedback and tells you to go back and improve something you have to do just that and work your very hardest when you try to improve. Last year on the New Jersey Assessment of Skills and Knowledge, which is the state test, I scored a two according to the writing rubric and with a month of work I am already passing the test.

Anibal Goytio
Ridge Street School

## The Wind Makes Me Smarter

It blows cold kisses in the October night. It blows away the leaves without a fight. What is this cold kiss blowing source it is the wind.

   The wind whistles a song in my ears on my way to school. It slaps me in the face, trying to keep me cool. When the wind does its dance, the leaves follow.

   They follow as if they were a bunch of children following the scent of cookies. That is what the wind does every day. And that is how the wind plays. I get smarter by letting the wind take my mind's troubles away.

Sienna Camacho
Dr. E. Alma Flagg School

## How Smart Am I?

How smart am I?

When reading books some tell no lie

Read books some torn pages

Never do that because the book ages

School is for learning and thinking

If you never do that your brain starts shrinking

Some come to learn, some come for sports

Some receive good or bad reports

I will ask again, "How smart am I?"

When people say that it makes me try

When some hear it they start to cry

For those reasons it's why I thrive

To read more books to make me wise.

Dakell Bryant
Newton Street School

# What I Think About Being Smarter

Willingness seems to be the notion that revolves around my mind as I think about someone who wants to become smarter. You need to be willing to listen and learn. You need to be open to constructive criticism. Learn from your mistakes and don't criticize others negatively. This reminds me of Isaac Newton's third law of motion, which states, "for every action there is an equal but opposite reaction." This implies that for everything you do there will always be a consequence whether positive or negative. Therefore, if you are willing and open, the reaction will be that you will become smarter.

I remember my mom once told me "If you don't fall, how will you know how to get up?" This suggests that if you don't make mistakes, how will you learn? Nobody's perfect so we are going to make mistakes, but make them worth it and learn from them.

Also, to become smarter you need to be a lifelong learner. Don't have the mentality that you already learned enough because you can always learn something new. When I think of becoming smarter I think: hard work and dedication. Don't you?

To me, becoming smarter means to give it all you've got and never give up. I have worked really hard to become smart. I'm dedicated and I never give up. I learn from my mistakes and every time my intelligent teacher tells me that I need to enhance something, I go and do that again and make sure it's better.

Benjamin Pimentel
Ridge Street School

# Smarter

"Prior knowledge" seems to be the solitary notion that fixated itself and revolved around my intellect when I decided that I was going to participate in writing what it means to be smarter. What it means to me is knowledge and better academic achievement.

As a student, I have learned to value the belief: "Education is the key to success."  My interpretation of this adage is that if you are smart and you enter a good high school and college you will be successful in life. In addition, becoming smart means more participation and you can even become a model for other kids in your class. What I have done to become smarter is that I have been studying and paying close attention when my teacher has been teaching.

I paid attention in class and look, I became smart. Why can't you?

Yaideliz Acevedo
Ridge Street School

# After School Programs

I imagine students leaving school and going home and watching TV and playing video games without opening a book until it's almost time for bed. I wish the state would mandate after school programs that would help students academically learn the process of applying good study habits, using resources, and utilizing valuable time: all keys to becoming smarter!

If they did, kids could learn and understand the assignment that their teachers give them. When students don't participate in other activities they won't understand the processes of what they're suppose to do in real life. Without education, you will not get anywhere in life.

Second, kids would be excited because of the educational field trips and the experiences that go along with it. The learning that we do in the program would be symbolic of the hard work and dedication that we strive for during the school year. I can speak from experience about an after school program because I am a product of what it is like to be a part of a great educational program. This after school program that I participated in, along with the help of Ms. Pagan, has helped me with my grades, and has improved my writing as well as being a beneficial tool for my other subjects.

Finally, if students attended a state mandated after school program, it would keep parents in their jobs. Parents would not have to worry about leaving work to pick up their children because they would be in proper hands.

John Perez
Ridge Street School

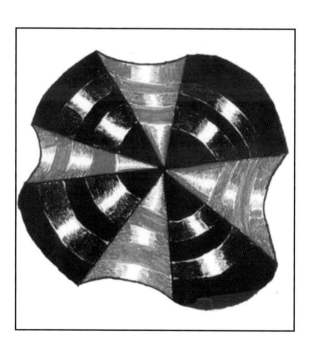

Jeffrey Decen
Dr. William H. Horton School

# Who Am I?

My favorite colors are pink and purple.
My favorite foods are chicken, cheese broccoli and macaroni and cheese.
I love to sing.
I love to draw.
I am a brave little girl.
I am a woman of God and I am 12 years of age.
I love to color.
I love to write.
I love to read.
Some say I am a geek for science, but I say I am gifted.
I am a B/C student.
I am smart yet becoming smarter
I don't come to school to make friends; I come to learn.
I am Shanyah Files.

Shanyah Files
Newton Street School


# The Way to Success

No drugs
No violence
No fighting
Be brave
Be smart
Be intelligent
Like my grandmother says, "Reach for the stars because if you fall, you'll land on a cloud."
I'm not trying to tell you what to do just how to do it.
I'm telling you how we can fix the future and change the world because the future is in our hand.

Imani Smith-Scott
Newton Street School

# Smarter

What makes a person smarter? I believe that you become smarter by studying what you know and relating it to your everyday life experiences. I agree with Dr. Carl Sagan when he said, "Knowing a great deal is not the same as being smart; intelligence is not information alone but also judgment, the manner in which information is collected and used." When you read a book or learn how to apply your knowledge in your life, you become more articulate, your vocabulary increases, and you are wise about topics you didn't understand before. As you grow older, there are more opportunities for you to succeed but you must also continue your education and be consistent. Creativity and imagination also help you retain information. They help you enjoy what you learn and look for ways in which the information can be used. Another person that I admire for his perseverance and his dedication towards education is Dr. Martin Luther King, Jr. He said, "The function of education is to teach one to think intensively and to think critically...Intelligence plus character—that is the goal of true education."

I believe that being smart is very important but what is more important is to always try your best. I don't believe that anyone is born smart. We must all work hard and try our best to become smart as we learn something new every day. It has been difficult for me to work hard and learn new things. However, I am trying my very best because when I get older I want to succeed and go to college. I want to try my best to follow my dreams and to graduate. I really admire my mom because she learned English, worked hard and graduated from college. She always tells me that it was hard to learn a new language and go to college at the same time. However, she tried her best and never gave up. Now she is a resource teacher and she says she is still learning every day and trying her best. I am always trying my best because as long as you don't give up on your dreams and continue to have aspirations, you will succeed.

In my opinion, you should always work hard, learn all of the things you can and believe that you can do anything in life if you put your mind to it. I would like to finish with a quote, "Every worthwhile accomplishment, big or little, has its stages of drudgery and triumph; a beginning, a struggle, and a victory." This implies that where there's a will there's a way.

Wouldn't you like to succeed and achieve your goals with determination and wisdom?

Kaitlyn Rios
Ridge Street School

## I Am

Beautiful
Strong
Pretty
Caring
Kind
Lovely
Brave
Talkative
Athletic
Sporty
I have a love for math, science and reading books.
But most of all I love my education.
I am smart
I am Yasmine Traynham

Yasmine Traynham
Newton Street School

## Marques

<u>Value</u>
It is valuable for me to pick up trash off the ground because trash causes destruction.
<u>Obstacle</u>
My biggest obstacle was when my father asked me if I wanted to live with him, because I am living with my mother.
<u>Goal</u>
My goal is to be a football player. The football team I want to play for is the Eagles because the Eagles are my favorite team.

Value + Obstacle + Goal = Smarter

Marques Cannon
Chancellor Avenue School

# I Grow Smarter

*I grow smarter by using my writing skills. I like to do creative writing. I like to talk about things that are important to teenagers like love and happiness. I model my writing after the love stories I read.*

Yazmira Cano
Dr. E. Alma Flagg School

## Smarter

Imagine papers are flying, notebooks are falling, and the computer is stuck on games from 3:00 – 9:00 p.m. A student is playing games on their computer and does not pay attention to their homework. At ten that night, the student rushes through homework and doesn't check it over. Is that what being smarter means to you? Well, not to me.

When I think of smarter, motivation comes to mind. Smart, to me, implies that a person will grow and become a lifelong learner. A student must be willing to be open for feedback from teachers and students. That's a good way to enhance your work.

Students that are attentive to their work and put in major effort, tend to be smarter. This isn't just a theory. It is reliable, consistent and data driven evidence. Imagine a student with straight A's who always pays attention in class. When it comes to peer editing, the student takes his time to improve his writing by fixing errors and improving the work. I think that being smart isn't only about getting good grades; it's also about working to your full potential and putting in effort.

I demonstrate that I am smarter by elaborating on my ideas in writing and in other subjects as well. I do my job and give 100% of my effort. That's the main part. I always like to improve my writing. I gaze at my writing and search for errors and adjust my paper so it is a higher quality. When my work is done, I can tell because it smiles from ear to ear at me showing its pride and contentment. That makes me proud. Many times I improve my writing from a four to a five or a six on the rubric. Outstanding, huh?

When our class puts in the hard work like doing extra credit, it symbolizes that we are smarter. Like the old saying goes, "It's better to add ingredients than to just cook the chicken." This suggests that you should add effort, not just worry about grades. It's not enough to just do homework everyday. Being smarter infers that you show work and take time to improve. This is what smarter means to me.

What does being smarter mean to you?

Kiana Perez
Ridge Street School

# What Happened to Me When I Was a Little Girl?

When I was a little girl, I lost my grandmother. My grandmother and I were very cool together. She was the best grandmother I ever had. When my grandmother died, I thought I lost everything. Every day, I would cry my heart out.

I was named after my grandmother. When my brothers and sisters and I were younger, we would go to her house every day after school. My grandmother meant everything to me. When I found out that I would not see her anymore that hurt me badly.

It was so bad that my mom thought something was wrong with me because no one could talk to me. I would not eat and I couldn't sleep. My heart just felt like it was in pieces.

One day, my father came up to me. (It was his mother that died, so he was more heartbroken than me). He explained what happened. He said, "People have to die. God wanted her. God wanted her to come to Him." My father and I had to get through that together. After that day, when my father and I would come together, we would think about all the happy memories we had with her. We had to go on with our lives. My dad and I had to be strong and not worry anymore about what happened.

We became stronger and better. Now, when we sit down and talk about my grandmother, we also talk about when my dad was a little boy and what we liked best about her. It was very heartbreaking for me to go through this as a little girl. I am thirteen years old now and I know a little more about how life works and what goes on. Although my grandmother is gone, I still have my other grandmother. She is wonderful to me!

Helen Solomon
McKinley School


# Smart Poem

Smart peas would find it rather odd
To be alone inside a pod
The smart peas like to hang out with their friends
For them the party never ends.
Can you see how smart the peas are?
Count up all the peas
It will be a breeze.
But the smart thing is to do your work and party last.

Aniyah Arrington
Newton Street School

# Smarter

Personal responsibility is the word I thought of when asked what it means to be smarter. To me, it implies a great amount of effort is required to get into a beneficial high school or a college. Education is to learning as prior knowledge is to smarter. I learned that some people's minds are like sponges. They can absorb all the knowledge and they can get motivated. Sometimes when we're in class and our teacher teaches us a new subject, I think to myself, "I can learn and do this." Sometimes I feel the adrenalin race rapidly through my veins just because I know I can learn something as easily as taking candy from a baby.

Learning is like riding a bike because you may mess up and fall down but you can always get up and try again until it is perfect. I believe I have self-confidence and I show it by pushing myself to the next level of learning.

I remember when my friends and I bolted into the classroom for the very first day and I sat next to my two best friends, Karina and Kiana. At the beginning of the year, I started talking a bunch and didn't complete all my assignments or homework. Mr. Lichten moved me up front because he felt my friends were a huge distraction. I listened a whole lot more in the front.

After Mr. Lichten moved me, I tended to take control of my actions and tried not to converse with the students who surrounded me. I was a quiet as a mouse. I also showed how I was responsible by being quiet, having self-control, not being distracted and putting my education first. Now I am gladly becoming smarter, not only by doing my work, but by showing it to others.

I have a lot of things to do in order to become smarter, starting now. I remember the quote: "Education is the key to success that unlocks all doors." This implies that education can unlock all possibilities for you. What it has taught me is when I moved to the front and listened, my homework was completed, my class work was outstanding, my behavior was amazing, and my grades were perfect.

What have you learned about being smarter? I learned that education is not boring if you really try and if you don't give yourself opportunities, you won't get anywhere in life.

Gabrielle Rosario
Ridge Street School

## The Smarter Me

My favorite book is, "The Skin I'm In." It allowed my mind to travel and me to see myself. I am inspired to make good grades. It's my goal and desire to get nothing less than a B.

My favorite subjects in school are math and science. Some say I think I know it all, but I say I am an intelligent Black male who speaks his mind.

This is the smarter me. I am Robert Williams.

Robert Williams
Newton Street School

## Smarter

Excited comes to my mind when I imagine being smarter. What it means to be smarter to me is to try my best in all subjects. During the first day of school my excellent writing teacher, Mr. Lichten, told our class all these new writing techniques we didn't even know. Like interdisciplinary, symbolism, word lead and now I'm trying to know about Howard Gardner and his theory about multiple intelligences, which teaches us how to use a variety of modalities by integrating all subjects into my writing.

I am smarter when I use these techniques in my writing. So far, I'm getting three's and four's in my writing. Every day, I improve. Now, I'm better at it. I show my irony writing to my teacher, Mr. Lichten and his jaw drops to the floor. He always says, "Believe and you will achieve." I have learned that if you do something and put your effort into it then you can go for it and achieve it.

Ultimately, what I have done to become smarter is by adding more techniques to my writing. I'm putting in more similes, transitions, and hyperboles. I learned these words like a snap of a finger.

Smart...Smarter.

Bryan Rosario
Ridge Street School

## The Way the World Works

People work, eat, sleep, and think.

Some people fall into failure others into success.

Where you fall depends on you.

Things go up, down, around and around as the universe orbits.

When you grow up be a shining star.

That is how the world works.

Ha-Leem Young
Newton Street School


## Danaya

Can your personality traits make you smarter?

I am a loving and caring person. I love animals. I hate to see them die because it hurts me very, very much. It makes me want to cry. My best friend says she enjoys me because I care about animals very much. The reason why I care about animals is because I have a dog of my own.

This is what I have done to value the world: I recycle and I give money to poor people who don't have any clothes or houses. When I help others, I feel confident because it is very nice to share. As a goal, I would like to get good grades and pay attention in school and graduate. When I grow up, I want to be a veterinarian because I love animals.

The important quote that inspires me is President Obama's campaign slogan, "Yes We Can." When we were in school taking the NJASK test, my teacher would tell us "yes we can" when we tried to pass the tests. She said, "If you work hard and put your minds to the work, you can pass." Every time I am doing my work, I always think about what my teacher told me.

Danaya Simmons
Chancellor Avenue School

**Are You Smarter?**

**S** — uper
**M** — ature
**A** — dventurous
**R** — eal
**T** — rustworthy
**E** — ager
**R** — ewarded

Javier Fernandez-Martinez
Newton Street School

**Smarter**

What does it take to become smarter?  Smarter can imply many things. I think that there is one way to become smarter—be dedicated in school.

I think that's the best way because if you are dedicated in school you will learn more. Then you will be as smart as a rocket scientist. If you always pay attention in class you can be the smartest person in the universe. This reminds me of the quote, "Education is the key to success."  My interpretation of this quote is without a beneficial education you can't have a good life.

Also, you have to become open-minded because you will have more knowledge on what to improve upon. This reminds me of what I learned in science class about Isaac Newton's three laws of motion; specifically, the third law which states, "For every action there is an equal but opposite reaction."  This implies that for everything you do there is a positive or negative consequence. This can relate to what I was saying earlier because if you care about your education you can become successful and that is a positive consequence.

A beneficial education can make you successful. I suggest that everyone should care for their education.

Christian Caban
Ridge Street School

# "Smarter: It's Something You Become"

I honestly think that when you put your effort and ambition into something, you will become more intelligent in your studies and school work. Not only do you have to put forth effort, but also show honor and dignity in yourself. What I mean by this is that in order to become a "smarter" person, it's not just a contest on whether or not you're intelligent, it's putting everything you have into something that's worthwhile.

Personally, I think I'm smarter because even if I'm not excited to do anything, I still have persistence. Smart shouts in my face: "Believe in yourself, and you can achieve!"

The thing I did to become smarter was actually surprising. It was a brisk, breezy Friday afternoon at around 2:35 p.m. The winds whipped throughout the sidewalks of Ridge Street. Swish! Swish! The immaculate sun was hidden behind the marshmallow clouds. I heard the laughter of children already outside playing hopscotch. I saw my homeroom teacher, Mrs. Witsch, handing out everyone's report card. As soon as she handed me mine, I read aloud my grades for only myself to hear.

"Writing: A, Science: A, Math: B, Social Studies: C!!!! I got a C in the easiest subject?!" Never in my life had I received anything lower than a B. Never in my life. But months later, I learned my lesson and went from a C to an A. I never slacked off from that day forward. All in all, I learned, "Believe and you will achieve." From my point of view, this implies that if you believe and set high standards in life, you will achieve in the long run.

Destiny Duprey
Ridge Street School

# Practice Makes Better

I love basketball. That's my favorite sport. I play basketball every day. When I grow up, I want to be a basketball player. I started playing basketball when I was five years old and I just stuck with it all my life. I choose basketball for the exciting and creative ways players dunk, cross, and shoot on the court. I practice a lot in the gym every day after school. I keep my grades up so that I can stay on the basketball team. I am a smarter basketball player because I always practice after school in the gym.

Vincent Davis
McKinley School

Jocelyn Zapata, McKinley School

## Smarter

Dedication was the first word that came to mind when I was recently pondering the question, "What does it mean to you to become smarter?" What do you think? Well, I will now provide you with my opinion.

Personally, I think that becoming smarter implies that you have to have words, persistence and confidence constantly in your cerebellum. It means that you are always ready to try your hardest. It suggests that you strive to be the best and not to settle for anything less. When you are dedicated to what you are doing your ambition forces you to keep on trying and never give up; even if you fail the first time. Even if you fail the first time, you can always learn from your mistakes. At first, I thought that only students who always get high grades were smart; however, I was wrong. They may get excellent grades but those students who study and do their best are smarter because they know that doing this will get them somewhere.

Just imagine students in classes sitting at their desks raising their hands for every question and being as hard-working as bees constructing their hives. They are doing this just to increase their knowledge because they are aware that being smarter signifies that you are giving 100%. This leads to a superior future because in order to succeed in life you need to have a good education. Doesn't this thought just make your jaw drop to the ground? Imagine seeing how motivated students would be just because they know what becoming smarter indicates or means.

The question, what does becoming smarter mean to you, really got me thinking about something. I always had those two words, persistence and confidence, in my cranium and I have been learning more and more.

*(continued)*

First, I focus on what I am doing and always give 100% in what I am doing. Secondly, I always believe in myself and have persistence. I always think to myself that I am smart but I can do better. I push myself, which helps me get even smarter. I am smarter because I believe. I can learn anything and even if I have trouble with something, I still practice constantly and BAM! I eventually understand it. Also, in order to get smarter I am always confident in myself and have positive thoughts by always saying to myself that one day I can be as smart as Albert Einstein. I am smarter because I learn from repetition because when I do something, I always do it over and over again and it goes into my long-term memory, which makes me remember it and have more knowledge.

I believe that I am smarter because I do try to be the best of the best. I also carry a charm that my mother gave me, which is symbolic of hard work. This charm helps me remember that you get smarter with hard work, persistence, dedication, and confidence. My father once told me, "Education is the key to success that unlocks all doors." This quote implies that the only way you will succeed in life, reach your ambition and have more options in your future is through your education. I keep this in my mind because I have to push myself in order to learn and get smarter, and doing this will help me in my future. Not only do I do this, I also get constructive criticism from my fellow classmates to improve anything I am doing. This is extremely helpful because when peer editing I get feedback from my peers about things I can improve so that I can get even better in what I am doing. I am also responsible and study for all my tests. I take each test as seriously as a President's meeting.

All in all, thinking smarter taught me, "Believe and you will achieve." If you have positive thoughts and give 100% effort in what you are doing, you will end up getting something positive out of it. When I am brighter, I end up getting even smarter because with these positive thoughts I try even harder.

Sheina Rivera (writing and illustration)
Ridge Street School

# Smart

In my opinion, I think smart suggests that you have to study for tests and just try the best you can. You have to be motivated.

On a cold, breezy autumn day, the sun was smiling down on me from ear to ear. I could almost smell the aroma of my breakfast, which included chocolate chip pancakes with maple syrup, fried eggs, and bacon. I was taking one of the biggest writing tests I ever took. As I was taking the test, all I could hear was the clock saying Tick Tock!  Tick Tock!

Whenever I take a test, I have this special lucky necklace that is shaped like a horseshoe. This necklace is symbolic to me because it helps me remember to do my very best.

When Mr. Lichten finished grading the test and gave it back to me, I was as anxious as a child on Christmas waiting to open gifts. I could feel the adrenaline going through my veins. When the results came in, I got a 100%. I was as elated as a puppy with a brand new bone.

My action of studying resulted in a reaction: an outstanding grade. This shows I am smarter because I used to get very low grades. I didn't study. But now that I do and use my prior knowledge, I pass.

In the future, I would like to go to Arts High School and go to Harvard University. In order for me to do that, I will have to work on being smarter and try my very best.

All in all, I learned that "education is simply the soul of a society as it passes from one generation to another." This implies that education is important in your life because without it you can't pass your education on to the next generation.

Brianna Perez (writing and illustration)
Ridge Street School

# What Does It Mean to You to Become Smarter?

What does it mean to you to become smarter? Well, when I think of smart, I think of bright, hard working, intelligent students and people. I, myself, being one of those mentioned above, know what it means to be and become smarter. First of all, you need to be attentive, willing to learn and to take in all the information you can grasp. But the learning doesn't stop in the classroom. That's what separates smart people from lifelong learners. Lifelong learners never halt their education only because it's taught in school. For example, they may go on the web and learn more things like math probability and algebra.

Almost every day you read and you might not even notice it. You may read a billboard on the highway, a sign on a door, or your textbook. You can never stop learning since there is no limit to intelligence. I call to mind a time when I used to check out five novels every week from the Newark Public Library. My vocabulary got larger and my reading skills went higher than the world's largest skyscraper, Taipei 101. It's very pertinent to have an education in this world right now. Everyone wants to have a lot of revenue and without an education; you will not succeed in life. All in all, to become smarter means that you are determined to become more intellectual.

To become smarter, you need the inspiration like Albert Einstein. Albert Einstein was a famous scientist who made the famous mathematical statement, $E=MC^2$. Einstein didn't get this just by sitting on a mahogany brown coach, watching his charcoal black TV with a bag of delicious, scrumptious bag of chips. He worked hard for this understanding and if you would like to become smarter, then you'll have to follow in his footsteps and work very hard too.

Louis Yepez
Ridge Street School

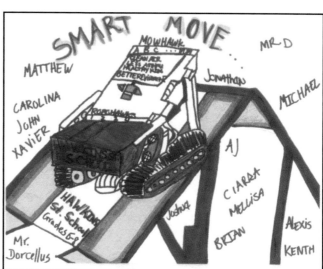

Carolina Frigato
Hawkins Street School

# Music = My Life

Music is my life. I love music. Music helps me with my emotions. When I'm sad, I listen to rock music. When I am crying, I listen to soul music. When I want to block someone out of my head, I put my headphones on and blast the music and go to sleep. Music is relaxing to me. I express myself with music. The way I live is musical. If I have a problem in my world, I turn to music.

I sing for a living. I love to sing. I play guitar and listen to the keys. I make songs from my life. If I hate what people think of me, I will write it in a song. Singing and music is in my blood, it is in my soul, it is in my body, my brain, my life, and it is in my heart. I love to sing and I love my music and no one is going to change that for me. And no one is going to ruin it for me. I love music.

Music is me!

Samira Perez
Dr. E. Alma Flagg School

# Celebrate Life

It was a hot sunny Christmas day in Puerto Rico when the kooky sounds of roosters interrupted my slumber. I awoke fascinated to still be in my grandma's house. I walked immediately across the solemn room to the fresh smelling, brightly lit bathroom. I was zestfully clean and beyond excited to join my family in the kitchen. The aroma of the morning's coffee being brewed and the scent of the oatmeal, platanos with ham and eggs being cooked was mouth watering.

Before I knew it, the sun was setting and evening was soon approaching. My hair was nicely set and my dress was impeccable. I was ready to celebrate.

Midnight...after much anticipation the clock finally struck 12. The music, talk, and laughter at no time paused. My family and friends were having a great time. I was having a great time too. Of course though the time had finally arrived and inevitably it was time to open gifts! All my gifts were great but the most memorable gift of all was when moments later we realized my cousin's dog had given birth to four gorgeous puppies! That was the greatest gift of all. It's funny how life's experiences teach us valuable lessons.

Christmas 2008 was definitely an unforgettable Christmas. I learned how our experiences can make us smarter.

Kassandra M. Ramos
Rafael Hernandez School

# The Fatal Accident

It was a gloomy dark day. I was cold and had goose bumps all over my arms. Something inside of me warned me that something bad was going to happen. I will never forget that unfaithful day.

The date was Friday, March 26, 2006. I felt my stomach twisting with fear. Time was flashing before my eyes. It was 1:55 p.m. and I was in the middle of gym class, when to my surprise, my sister and I were urgently sent to the main office with our book bags and coats. As I ran down the stairs, I pictured terrible things.

Sadly, as I approached the office, I saw my mother crying. Her cheeks were red like a tomato!  She was shaking with fear. The closer I was, the more I could see my homeroom teacher, Mrs. Basile with my mom at the office. Mrs. Basile is a very nice teacher. She has blue eyes, brown hair and a peachy skin tone. "Take care of your mother, she is really feeling down!" said Mrs. Basile. I felt my heart sink when I saw tears rushing down my mother's cheeks. I didn't know what to do.

The day got worse!  Suddenly it started to snow and my mom, sisters and I rushed to the car. Out of the blue, my older sister asked if someone died. Then my twin sister tried to guess who it was. Finally, she asked, "Tio Guichy?" and my mom started crying even more. Soon after, my mom started to speed and it was as if we were flying through the streets. I told my mother to take a deep breath so we could get home safely.

After awhile I broke down. "How did he die?" I asked. "He got into an accident with his truck," I heard someone say. He was driving a cement truck, when a screw snapped from the back where the cement was mixing. He was going up a hill and the weight of the cement tilted the truck sideways and started to pull the truck down a steep hill. He tried to jump out but the truck pulled him down the hill crushing him on the way down. The news was devastating and will always be imprinted in my life.

Tio's death taught us that it is important to love those that are close to us while they are here. You never know when you may never get the chance again. Tio Guichy was only 43 years old. We called him Tio. He was my mom's favorite uncle. He was a very loving and fun person to be around. Rest in peace, Tio. We will never forget you.

Dayanara Ocasio
Rafael Hernandez School

## Smarter

**S** – Studying is the key to success

**M** – Motivation keeps me going

**A** – Ask for help

**R** – Raise my scores

**T** – Teachers are wonderful

**E** – Exercise my mind

**R** – Reading is fundamental

Gisselle Santiago
Avon Avenue School

## Smarter?

The question is, "What does it mean to you to become smarter?" Open-minded is the word that comes to my mind because your mind has to be open to all the new learning experiences that come your way. Accepting these opportunities instead of neglecting them or throwing them away will unlock new possibilities for the future. You require an education in order to get somewhere in life. If you don't accept the learning experiences, you won't get anywhere in life.

I know a lot of ways to show that I am smarter. I received a glowing note from my teacher stating that I obtained an A average in writing, science, health, and social studies so far. This note was symbolic of my hard work and dedication. I recall my reading teacher, Ms. Perez was checking my homework and she said, "You're a good student." I know I am because I always complete all my homework.

I've done a multitude of things to make myself more knowledgeable. I reach and work to accomplish 100% of my responsibility in school so I can achieve a 4.0 GPA. Also, I learned to enhance my writing with word leads and rich vocabulary.

These are essential to making a person smarter.

Damian Garcia
Ridge Street School

### Here's What Smarter Means to Me!

**S**olve problems that are in front of you!
**M**ake a good choice!
**A**sk lots of educated questions!
**R**ead books that will help you learn and try something new!
**T**ry as hard as you can!
**E**dit your work!
**R**emember what your teachers and parents tell you!

Andrea Holley
Mt. Vernon School

### My Great Birthday

It was a crisp Thursday morning. The bright sunlight was beaming in my face until I heard a loud startling noise, "BOOM!" My brother was in my room. Still acting like I was asleep I felt him coming closer. Then I heard a screech, "Surprise, Happy Birthday, Ashley!"

It was my 13th birthday. I didn't feel different nor did I look any different. Did I get taller? Yeah, I guess but that was all I got, taller! That's it? I thought to myself, "It's my birthday. I'm getting older so this should be fun." I was right! It was fun! My cousins, aunts, uncles, everyone, even two of my best friends came. All at once, I heard "Birthday Punches!" Then the inevitable punches on each arm—one friend on one arm, another on the other arm.

Suddenly, "Happy Birthday," a low gentle voice said. It was my grandmother! I ran up to her and gave her a big hug. It truly was the best birthday ever.

I felt so happy that day. I've never been so happy like that before! It wasn't about presents or getting what I wanted. It was about everyone having a great time dancing and playing games. It truly, truly was the best birthday of my life. I enjoyed everything about it. For my next birthday, well, I don't care as long as I have my family with me!!

Ashley Vega
Rafael Hernandez School

## Smarter

**S**     study long and hard

    **M**     math is my favorite subject

        **A**     always believe in myself

            **R**     reading inspires me

                **T**     teaching makes learning fun

                    **E**     educating my mind

                        **R**     ready for the world

Ashley Rosa
Avon Avenue School


## SMARTER

**S** – Smart Kids

**M** – Math binders organized

**A** – A's on report cards

**R** – Ready for school on time

**T** – Trying your best

**E** – Everybody works

**R** – Reading all the time

Jamal French
Avon Avenue School

## Smarter

**S**     Smart kid
**M**     Math is good
**A**     All were paying attention
**R**     Reading is good
**T**     Time to learn
**E**     Eat a healthy breakfast
**R**     Read

Jahad Lyde
Avon Avenue School

## Rafael Hernandez:  The Place to Be!

Do you know where students hang out in my community?  You probably don't know but kids in my neighborhood know. It's at Rafael Hernandez!  It's a school located at 345 Broadway in Newark, NJ. Why Rafael Hernandez, you say?  Well, it's a huge place! Our playground covers a lot of ground where you can run freely. No one can tell you to go away like they do in some other places. It is open to anyone in the community. I always see other kids from other schools hanging out talking with their friends about the good times he or she had at Rafael Hernandez. This school is truly the place to be.

Rafael Hernandez is very important to me because it's where I get my education. It's where I begin my journey of 1,000 miles. It's where I meet great teachers who teach me valuable lessons. It's where opportunities come to take me in a specific direction. From joining the debate team and the robotics team, my name will be heard throughout this country and it all began at Rafael Hernandez.

Rafael Hernandez is important to the community because it's a children's hang out spot. There are not many safe hang out spots in the neighborhood. Many kids live near Rafael Hernandez and if they have a friend, they might want to socialize during the weekends so they meet up there. Imagine if Rafael Hernandez was never built!  These kids would stay in their house all day, bored. That life stinks!  These kids need to go out there to be who they are...kids!  Children need to be active and have a social life. Rafael Hernandez is an important place in the community.

The students, the community, and I know that Rafael Hernandez is the place to be. Hernandez is the place for kids to hang out in the community and the place for me to begin my journey of 1,000 miles. Children should be given the opportunity to be who they are and do what they enjoy, such as playing games and making friends.

Rafael Hernandez is the perfect place for any child in my community.

Luis Cruz
Rafael Hernandez School

# Hang Out

A place in my neighborhood where kids and teenagers can hang out is called the Boys and Girls Club. It is a place where everyone can hang out and just be themselves. We can play basketball, baseball, or even go swimming. There are game machines in the club as well. It is a very fun place to be and a lot of kids go there every day.

The Boys and Girls Club means a lot to me. It is a place that my friends and I go to hang out. We can relax and just hang out. We don't have to worry about school or homework! I like to go on the computer and play the game machines. Even swimming at the Boys and Girls Club is fun. One time my friend and I were having a swimming contest and even though she won (because she cheated), I still had fun!

At the Boys and Girls Club I see everyone having fun and enjoying their time there. I see that parents don't have a problem with their children spending time there because it is a fun and smart place to be. The Boys and Girls Club is safe and they even have teachers there to help the kids with their homework or projects. I think the Boys and Girls Club is a good place for kids and teenagers to hang out and have fun. The parents think it's a good place for their kids to be active and learn new things. The local police like the Boys and Girls Club because it's an excellent place for kids to spend time instead of getting into trouble on the streets.

In closing, I think the Boys and Girls Club is a very cool place where kids and teens should spend a lot of time. It is even a place to play sports too. I know I have fun going to the Boys and Girls Club!

Jada Obesso
Rafael Hernandez School

Hassan Haywood

Hawthorne Avenue School

# I Hate Uniforms

Today I woke up and the sun was in my eyes. I didn't want to put on those ugly uniforms. Every time I look at those uniforms it makes me want to throw up. The boring khaki pants and the plain burgundy shirt are not my style.

Before I went to school I went to my cousin's house. She lives down the street from me, but she goes to a different school. When I got there she was ready to walk me to school.

She was walking down the street when I said, "Your school colors are pretty!" "Well your uniform is ugly!" She responded.

As we were walking to school, I was so aggravated. I felt so ashamed and awful that she would really put me down like that. After school I was looking for my sister and I couldn't find her because everyone was wearing the same clothes! Guess what? She was standing right in front of my face. When I got home I decided to write in my diary to let out all my emotions about these uniforms.

*September 12, 2009*

*Dear Diary,*

*I'm sorry for acting like a brat but wearing my normal clothes is the only way I can express myself. Also, it helps me bring out my beauty for fashion. Wearing my regular clothes shows everyone who I am.*

*Love,*
*India*

Just then the doorbell rang and I went to answer it.

"Who is it?" I yelled through the door.

"Your auntie," replied my aunt.

As soon as I opened the door my auntie said, "Ohhhhh, you look so cute in your uniform!" From then on I kept getting compliments on my uniform. Maybe uniforms aren't so bad after all.

India Martin
Rafael Hernandez School

## Don't Take Life For Granted

I'm a very happy outgoing young lady who has a positive can-do attitude at all times. At birth, I was adopted by my mother's biological cousin who is now my mother and I love her with all my heart. I thank her for being there for me. Through that experience, I have learned that life shouldn't be taken for granted.

My hobbies are going to the Newark Police Explorer Program that I attend every Wednesday after school. I like it because we have a lot of people from the Army and Newark City Hall that come and speak to us about important things that are going on in the outside world and what we'll be facing as we get older. I also enjoy the program because I get to work and earn community hours with special activities like community picnics, cancer walk marches, and a lot of other special events. I also attend dancing school and I take jazz classes every Thursday after school. I like it because I feel relaxed and that's what I like doing: RELAXING!

I hope to be a police officer or a music teacher in the future. I would enjoy working in society and trying my best to have my community feel safe and proud of their city. I would also enjoy working with children. So, if I become a music teacher I know I would be very loved by my students.

I have the power to help change society and make my community a better place. The focus should be on having free activities. Programs for teens such as additional sports programs would be helpful. I believe that if there are more positive things to keep youth busy and out of the streets, then there will be less violence and more hope for our younger children. Things will be much better.

Alexis Arpaio
McKinley School

## Friendship

Friendship is sitting in a room without talking and feeling it was the best conversation you've ever had. It's about you being there for one another through the ups and downs. Your friends being there means support, sister or brother. When you want to talk to someone, no betrayal in line to ruin the best thing in life that is free to me: FRIENDSHIP.

Alexandra Malave
Dr. William Horton School

# My First Award

I was so excited. The basketball tournament was tonight. I was upstairs in my room on my laptop listening to music. I could hear my aunt coming upstairs. "Are you still going to that tournament you keep talking about?" she asked.

I looked up to find her in her baseball uniform. It read "City Street."

"Oh did you have a game? Did you win?" I asked closing my laptop.

"Yeah we won a blowout, twenty-six to seven. Oh yeah, I almost forgot to tell you, your mom wants you downstairs."

"Mom, you wanted something?" I asked.

"Yeah, you have to leave; the tournament is starting in ten minutes. You uncle is outside to take you, now get going." She waved and smiled.

I nodded and went to the closet to get my jacket. My family's trophies were sitting on a shelf next to the closet. I stared right at the basketball trophy and said to myself, "I will have a trophy on that shelf. I will!" and I ran off to the car.

"Tournament huh," my uncle said as he drove.

"Yeah," I answered looking out the window.

"Nervous?" he asked.

"Yep," I nodded as we turned into the parking lot of the school, the tournament was held there. As I got out of the car, I kept on thinking back about the days I stayed out late in my backyard practicing and practicing my shooting, my dribbling, and my passing too. I knew that the next day my arms would hurt but I kept on practicing.

We walked into the gym of the school. I couldn't remember the name of the school, but it really didn't matter to me. I just wanted to be there. The place wasn't really filled with kids, just a few boys and one girl. The game went like this: it was boys vs. boys and girls vs. girls. Each person gets 25 shots, whoever shoots the most of the 25 wins, but there was a long strip of tape placed on the floor.

"You can't pass this line!" the score keeper pointed. I was up first because I picked heads and changed my mind to tails. I got a good look at the girl. Her hair was black and was pulled back into a ponytail. Her arms crossed, looking very serious. She wore a frown. The whole time I was there, I didn't remember her smiling at all. I knew it was bad news. I felt afraid, yet calm. So I just tried to wipe away my sweat.

I bounced the ball a few times before I began shooting. Three shots in and four missed.

"Come on Karen!" My uncle cheered.

I tried my very best but failed. I sat down watching the other girl shoot. She was good, if I have to say so myself. She missed a few shots, but she was still good. I was called to get up and look at our scores. She won, I knew it. Luckily she only won by two points, two points which I could have scored but didn't. My award was given to me. It read: **Second Place**. I jumped up and down, I was very excited.

"I won an award! I won an award!" I yelled.

People stared but I didn't care. At least I tried my best to get this far. I was so excited and happy to win this award. For the first time in my life an award was for me to keep. I won it. I just couldn't believe it!

Home at last. I immediately showed off my second place trophy. I looked up at my aunt while my mom took a good look at it.

"Good job! Try to go for first placed next time. OK?" She said.

I nodded. My mom gave me a big hug and my uncle cheered on. I walked over to the family trophy shelf and placed my winner next to the 1st place baseball and basketball trophies that my aunt won. I stared at her trophy, then back at mine.

"Next time I'm going for number one!" I said.

Karen Rios
Rafael Hernandez School

## I Have Learned

From the day that I realized it wasn't my fight
I became smarter through the day.
It was the most unbelievable sight
Dust in my eyes, was just a phase.
I learned that it was just dust on my shoulders
I just had to brush it away.
This made me smarter
To learn to take judgment
How to love and praise.
I have learned what getting smarter means
It means hard work, struggle, and confidence.
I didn't know this until now.
I learned to be forgiven for my bad deeds
I've called out mercy.
But the only person that could save me during this time filled with grief was me.
This is why I have chosen this path;
I've gone through too much to go back the way I was.
I learned now that I look at life with an outlook, an opinion.
I have learned to love back.
I have learned to love life.
I have learned to be smarter.

Steve Roopnarine
Dr. William H. Horton School

## Proving Them Wrong

Early one bright Monday morning at 8:00 a.m., I was getting ready for class. I remembered that I did not know how to spell my name. Everyone already knew how to spell half of their name. When the teacher told everyone to write their name, Mrs. Elf had to write my name for me. From that moment on I wanted to learn how to spell my name.

When school let out at the end of the day I overheard the teacher and the vice principal saying that I was dumb because I did not know how to spell my name and every other student knew how to spell their name. I was so mad.

Later that day I asked my sister "would you teach me how to spell my name?" She answered, yes, but only if I listen to her. I did as she asked, but usually she was going to say it too fast. When I arrived home I asked my mom if she would teach me how to spell my name. Mom replied, "Yes, I'll teach you how to spell your name." Mom wrote it on a piece of paper. I studied it for three hours like it was carrots on my plate for dinner. The next morning I was ready to go to school; ready to impress my teacher.

I arrived at school, looked at the building with the bright yellow sun in my face. I trudged up the stairs of the green funky smelling hallway. I started to walk to my desk in the back of the lemon scented class next to the blue beds and black TV above my head ready to write. The teacher asked everyone to spell their name like yesterday. Mrs. Elf was surprised when it was my turn to write my name. I wrote it perfectly!

Isiah Miller
15th Avenue School

Kenneth Barber

Dr. William H. Horton School

# Disaster in a Hospital

"Her appendix has burst inside of her and if she doesn't get surgery today there's not a possibility she will make it to tomorrow." Those were the words that came out of the doctor's mouth as he told my mother the reason that I had to have surgery. Well let me tell you how everything happened.

I was in bed tossing and turning, unable to sleep. My stomach was hurting and I felt dizzy. It was a weekday so I had to go to school. I got up around six in the morning to get ready but as soon as I stood up from the bed I felt weak and I could not walk as fast as I did before. I began to walk to my mother's room so that I could explain to her how I felt. When I entered her room my mother said, "Que te pasa?" which means "What's wrong?"

"No me siento bien. I don't feel good, my stomach has this pain that won't go away and I feel really dizzy." I told her.

"Go lie down and see if that helps," she responded. I headed back to my little messy room and lay on my full size bed that felt so uncomfortable at the moment. I got up and went to the big gold and brown living room and lay on the long brown couch but that didn't help. The pain got worse and I started to cry. My mom came out of her room and gave me some medicine, but all that did was make me throw up. That day I didn't go to school, instead I stayed home and layed in bed. I didn't want to eat anything, didn't want to drink anything. All I felt like doing was sleeping and lying in bed because I felt tired.

About two days later I didn't feel better, instead I got worse and I became pale white. My mom got scared and took me to the doctor.

We entered this big blue and white building that looked very familiar but different at the same time. A while later I noticed that it was the doctor's office. I had not been there for a long time. I guessed they had made some changes. I was getting sick and tired of being in that office because of all the little kids crying, running, and screaming, "Mommy, mommy, look, look."

When they called me into the room they told me to go in room number three and wait for my doctor. After a while Dr. Roberts walked in. First he asked me what was wrong, and then he checked me out to see if he could find out what was wrong with me. About ten minutes later he finally noticed what was wrong with me. The expression on his face changed completely. At first he had a nice big smile but after checking me, his smile turned upside down.

He slowly turned to my mother and said, "I am sorry but she needs to have surgery." My mom burst into tears.

He paused for a moment and then continued. "Her appendix has burst inside of her and if she doesn't get surgery today there's not a possibility she will make it to tomorrow," he said.

He asked my mother if she wanted him to call an ambulance, which my mother already knew I didn't like, so she said no.

When we walked out of the doctor's office my mother called my father and explained to him what had happened. She told him that she was going to take my sister to his house so that his wife could watch her while they went to the hospital.

On the way to my dad's house my mother would not stop crying and since she wouldn't stop my sister began.

When we got to my father's house my sister got out of the car and rang the doorbell. My stepmother opened the door. My sister hugged her and cried.

While in the car driving to the hospital I got more and more scared. The thought of having surgery scared me. I thought to myself what if I don't make it out of the surgery room alive. What if they make a mistake or do something they aren't supposed to and I die? So many thoughts went through my head but were eventually stopped by the tears running down my mom's cheeks as she told my stepfather what Dr. Roberts had told her.

My heart sank. It felt as if it came out of place and then went back in. My mom cried and cried and wouldn't stop.

When we got to Columbus Hospital my dad was already waiting for us to arrive. We entered the hospital and my mother went up to the main window and gave them my name. As soon as she said 'Clary' the woman told the nurse, "here she is," and they sat me down on a wheel chair and took me off to the emergency room. I was put in a room with a whole bunch of machines. While in that room they took samples of my blood, gave me a shot and took my temperature. They inserted the I.V. and then they told me to go and change into a robe looking thing.

When I finished putting the robe on I used the bathroom and flushed the toilet. "Flushhhhhhh." The sound of the toilet got me dizzy and I felt very weird.

When I got out of the bathroom my grandmother, father, stepmother, and mother were all waiting there—all sad, eyes full of tears. The weird sour milk smell made my stomach sick so I laid down and waited for whatever was next.

They took me into another room with my mother. They ran a few tests and then did a CAT scan. The nurse finally took me back to the room I was in before. To my surprise my surgeon was there. He introduced himself to me and then he explained to me how the surgery was going to go. After the explanation I got a little calmer because I knew that he wasn't going to let me die. Finally he left to change into his uniform. My mom and dad talked to me. They told me I shouldn't worry about anything because I was going to be okay. The truth was I wasn't really that worried; they were the ones who were.

A few minutes later they took me to the surgery room. There they let me talk to my parents.

They told me "te quiero mucho," which means I love you,

I told them not to worry because I was going to be okay.

About five minutes later the surgeon's helper came and rolled me away on the bed. We went to level three where the surgery room was. When we got there they told my family to wait for me in the waiting room.

We went through the double doors. As soon as we entered the room I got really tired and I couldn't stand that old nasty rusty smell that felt as if it came from between the walls. I couldn't keep my eyes open. All I remembered was really bright lights, white walls, the rusty smell, and a lot of breathing machines and nurses that were cleaning these tools that looked like real long needles, about two minutes after I was in the room I fell asleep.

About an hour and a half later I woke up and all I saw was this breathing mask on my face. I got scared but when I looked to my right I saw my mother. I got calm again. My father came in a few minutes later but then the nurse said that she was going to take me to my room which was 311B.

There my aunt, grandmother, father, and stepmother were waiting for me. But since I didn't get any sleep in those days that I was at home when I got back to my room I immediately fell asleep.

The next day the nurse came in to check my temperature and give me a blood test. She also told my father that they were going to make me start walking so that I could get used to walking. It took me about twenty five minutes to walk from my room to the security desk. After that I went back to my room.

Since it was a Sunday (family day) my uncle, his kids, and his wife were all there visiting me. Later on that night my cousins and my mom's workers came over and brought me balloons and teddy bears. I was happy. I felt so special. A lot of people really do care about me. Around six o'clock that day they asked everyone to leave because I needed to get some rest. They all said bye and then left.

That night I couldn't sleep because of the little boy that was on the other side of my room. He cried and cried from the pain that he had on his face from an ingrown hair that became a ball full of puss. So all I did was watch television and then around two in the morning I fell asleep.

The next morning the doctor woke me around six-thirty so that she could check my temperature and run a blood work activity. After that she gave me some medicine so that my fever could go down. Later on that day my mother and father switched shifts to watch me. My mother told my dad that she was going to go to the school I was attending that year so that she could tell my teacher what had happened and why I was going to be out of school for a couple of weeks.

About four hours later my mom returned from my school. She told me what had happened and how my teachers reacted to the matter that I was getting surgery and that I almost died. She told me that my literacy teacher began to cry. I kind of expected that because she is very sentimental. My mother told me that my math teacher told her he was going to pray for me and my science teacher said that she was going to have the class do some get well cards for me. When my mother told me this I was happy because one of my teachers actually cried for me.

Uhhh! Being in the hospital for so long was getting annoying. So I was anxious to go home when my doctor came in and told me that she was going to remove the stitches.

"Is it going to hurt?" I asked.

"It might hurt but just a little," she paused for a second and then said, "but you're a strong girl. I am sure you can handle it."

She began to take the stitches out one by one. It didn't hurt. All I felt was the tweezers pinching my skin each time. After she finished she told me, "Since I have pulled the stitches out now I have to pull the tube out."
I was a little nervous because I have heard in the past that it hurts when they pull on it.

"I am going to count to three and then I am going to pull," she said. "One, two." Whoosh! Everything in me felt as if it had moved. I felt hot then cold.

"Wow, I can't believe you didn't scream or anything. Most teenagers cry or scream because it hurts them. You're such a strong girl," she said.

I couldn't believe it. Now I didn't have the tube in me and now this meant that I could finally go home in a couple of days.

The next day my surgeon came to my room and said, "Wow, what are you still doing here?" "I don't know," I replied. "Well I do know they never told me that I could leave," I said.

He then asked me if I felt good enough to walk and if I felt strong enough to go home. I responded yes at least five times. I was sick and tired of being in that place just laying there doing nothing but sleeping and watching television. I couldn't move my right arm and I couldn't do much with my left arm.

The next day my surgeon came back and told me that I was safe to go home. I was so excited I got up and they told me that they had to remove the I.V. and then told my mother to sign a paper. My mom called my father and grandmother and they were all excited that I got to go home.

"Ahhhhhh! Home sweet home," I said to myself as I entered my apartment building.

When I got inside my apartment my mother told me that she was going to throw me a welcome home party the next day. I really didn't care about the party. I was just happy to be home. When my stepfather came home he had this box. He gave me the box and I ripped the wrapping paper off and inside was this beautiful blue Dell laptop.

"Yes, yes, yes! My own brand new laptop," I screamed.

Now no one can bother me when I am on the computer I thought.

The next day (Sunday) my grandmother woke me up and gave me some medicine then I took a shower and played on my laptop. About two hours later my big-headed cousins came over. I was so happy to see them. They hugged me but then backed off because they didn't want to hurt me. My aunt, grandmother, mom's friend, cousins, and stepfather came to my house. We listened to music, ate, and talked about me and my surgery. I had such a good time but then started feeling sleepy so my mom kicked everyone out. I went to sleep. That night I dreamed of waking up in Heaven but I never knew why.

About a week later I went back to school. My teachers and classmates were so happy to see me. They all gathered around me and asked me questions about the surgery and how I felt after it. I told them how hard it was for me to have the surgery and then have to get up and walk for my first time after surgery. I also told them how I couldn't move and how I felt being in that hospital for a week and how I couldn't move because of all the pain.

Now when I think back to the date November 7, 2009 I thank the man that did my surgery. I thank God because without them I could have died. I think I am lucky because the doctor told me usually you're not supposed to last more than two days with the poison inside of you because you can die. But me, Clary Leidy Rivera lasted three days with it and I am still living; that is why I thank God.

I tell everyone that asked me how I did it to never give up on yourself and stay strong and "God" will help you through everything and all your problems that you have in your life. Just like me, I stayed strong, and made it through everything.

Clary Rivera
15th Avenue School

# My Journey Into The Past—17th Century

Dear Diary,

   The court has ordered what is left of my family today as of October 28, 1762. Now I feel shame. Father has died of yellow fever at the age of 57. Mother cried through the whole ceremony of his burial. Madam Luna, my dear aunt, wore all black to the burial; everybody did except my mother. She was the only one who wore a white dress...her white wedding dress.

   The words of the preacher echo in my head, "we are gathered here today..." My mother screams continuously. My only sibling, Louise LoLette, born fresh six months does not understand what is happening. She looks at mother and to father's coffin that lays on the ground. Her green eyes are joyful though today is not a joyful day,

   When the burial is over, Madam Luna calls to her servants completely drenched of rain, to get her carriage. Madam Luna, mother, Louise, I, and the servants get in the carriage once it arrives. Slowly as the carriage moves I began to sleep.

   Finally...time...space. "Enjaiya" my dear aunt whispers as she cradles my mother; for I do not answer, for I will miss father.

Janaiya Lawrence
Dr. William H. Horton School

Jordeny Jordan

15th Avenue School

# A Forty!?

Have you ever done so well that the minute something slips your mind, it ruins your enter groove!? Hmpf! Well I've been there and done that! Three years ago, I was in the fourth grade, here at Fifteenth Avenue School, Ms. Flores's class. Every Friday we'd have to complete a quiz, a vocabulary quiz. And we'd already be prepared. That's how things went around there. We already knew what to do, when to do it, and how to do it. There were few complaints.

That year I'd considered it the most structured class of all. It was just so smooth. When the time came for us to accomplish our quiz, I, Charisma Lyles was unprepared for the first and only time! I reported to school that day, we had our morning meeting, reviewed the homework—hold on, before I get ahead of myself. I went a little too fast in my timeline. I woke up that morning a little late at about 7:54 ante meridian, to cold in my eyes and morning breath. Luckily, I showered the night before.

My sister, Al' Nesha had showered the night before as well. She was attending Fifteenth Avenue too. But had this "puberty" phase occurring, to where she had to be "extra-clean." I brush my teeth with Colgate, Oxi Clean with Baking Soda, twice. Next, I washed my face with a hot wash cloth and Black Aloe Soap with Shea Butter. The soap was lumpy, it smelled like a pair of new shoes. I quickly ironed my Vigoss Jeans and swiftly dressed myself.

I slipped on my, "All eyez on me!" t-shirt followed by my black sweater top with white cuffs and collar. I put on my red, black, and white Nike sneakers. I brushed the edges of my hair and greased them with "DAX" grease as well. I found myself trudging with great ferocity towards the door.

Now I still had to wait for Al' Nesha. That was a good five minutes I had to wait for her to get out of the shower after I was done. And the bad thing about it was that I had to wait a little longer for her to lotion, deodorize, and a bunch of other unnecessary refreshing that she does. Now it's about 8:09 a.m. She decides to choose now to fix her hair! Now she's spraying, parting, beveling, spraying, parting, beveling... Finally, she's finished. Now it's about 8:15 a.m. She has to find her bag, Geesh! Could it get any worse? She finds it! It's 8:18 a.m. We arrive at school. It's about 8:21 a.m. We were officially considered TARDY!

Now I'm caught up. I reported to class that day. Back to the "Ms. Flores" scented room; it was filled with the joyous smell of Ms. Flores. She had this sweet distinctive scent. We had our morning meeting, reviewed the homework, and completed our class work up until it was time to fill out our quiz. Now I knew this was no joy ride for me! Ms. Flores instructed us to align our desks into rows and columns and to put everything on our desks away except for a writing utensil. I sat down to complete my task. As I wished it to be five minutes later so that I could take a glance at the vocabulary chart before she covered it up.

Ms. Flores walked through each aisle passing out blank sheets of loose-leaf paper to each of us. On our tests we were informed to write a complete heading as we got our papers. And when it was time to begin we'd write our five vocabulary words without any misspellings. Next we had to define those five words as well. And to close the quiz up we had to write each word in a sensible sentence. We couldn't forget to number everything, or else it'll subtract points itself.

When completing the quiz you *had* to be on point, or you had a bad grade. If I were you I'd study and "check, check, and recheck" if I thought I was done with my quiz! Because all those points count and I guess this time something got in my way and threw me off! She shouted the words, "You may commence!" loud enough for everyone to hear.

While testing, I heard police and ambulance sirens outside the window. As the small white machine with black lines and numbers ticked on her desk, it ticked faster than you can say the, "T" sound! I began my quiz. I managed to complete the portion that contained writing the vocabulary words without being misspelled words in a breeze. As soon as it was time for me to complete the definition fragment, I began to break a sweat. My stomach dropped, my heart began to beat really fast.

And I immediately got frustrated. As I got further in the quiz my conscious grew more and more. It seemed to be getting harder and harder. All I could think about is, "How can I create five sentences when I barely know the five definitions?" The definitions were the toughest piece of the quiz.

In fact, I don't recall completing all of them. I don't know what came up that night that I couldn't study. Me! Of all people. Any other time I'd study; better yet I'd ace my test! So, you know the rest of that story. Yep! I didn't get to the sentence portion of my quiz.

This means I didn't complete the assignment. About 10 to 12 minutes passed nearest to 15 and I was still struggling on the definition piece. I then realized that all of my other classmates were wrapping the assignment up. And come to think of it, none of them were having difficulties as much as I was. If so, they were presenting themselves pretty sane.

I doubt it! There was no perplexity. With a big, fat, red, "F," in bold print. Ms. Flores called my house and my dad answered while my mom was at work. When my teacher called my house she stated she was a teacher from Fifteenth Avenue School. So my dad automatically knew only Al' Nesha and I attended Fifteenth Avenue. Then, as she continued explaining my grade; he assumed it was Al' Nesha because he had no thought in his right mind it was me.

When my mom got home from work, my father told my mom it was Al' Nesha. It was just a big misunderstanding. At 2:55 p.m. that day all students were dismissed. We had arrived home at about 3:05 p.m. Al' Nesha had no idea she was about to be in for a rude awakening.

When we got home my mother was upset and yelling at my brother about how Al' Nesha got a bad grade on her quiz. Al' Nesha eventually heard my mother hollering, so she wanted to see what was going on. Then my mother started yelling at her. Al' Nesha wondered what she did. As my mother went on and told her what happened screaming, "You know what happened, don't play crazy!" My father walked in from picking my little sister up from school and asked what happened. My mother explained what was going on and my dad agreed. Al' Nesha was still puzzled until my dad walked upstairs and told her why my mother was yelling at her. My mother said to Al' Nesha, "I don't know how you are going to do it, but you'd better figure out a way to increase that grade." By then, my mom had already calmed down. By the way, I didn't know what was going on, until I arrived at school the following Monday.

Ms. Flores' class was organized. The desks were in groups of four, the papers were stacked in a neat pile near the front door. The trash can was in the corner where you enter the threshold. In the beginning of the school year the place was nearly barren with the exception of papers, boxes of new notebooks and textbooks in the closet, books on the shelves, desks, chairs, etc. It almost seems as though she prepared the classroom over the summer.

Ms. Flores told me my grade at lunch time. I'd come up to help her grade the quizzes at lunch time. I had scored a forty! All I could do was stand there. While I stood there I thought about Friday when I was completing my quiz and when I got home of how my sister, Al' Nesha got blamed for my heavy duties. Then it all started to add up.

It was like a movie if I visualize it now in my recollection. I felt guilty. I didn't want to tell anyone anything because I was afraid of what would happen. I waited two weeks to come clean. Everyday I'd walk with Al' Nesha to school and she'd cry telling me she checked all her test scores and didn't get a forty. And one day I cried with her but I tried to hold back my tears because I hate to see people cry.

It seemed as though Monday came too soon. I had come upstairs with Ms. Flores to help decorate the bulletin boards at lunchtime. That's when I found out it was me who got the forty! I stood there in a state of shock, speechless. I thought to myself, "So I am what was wrong with the big misunderstanding in Nesha's punishment."

I felt so guilty that I caused this much trouble that I had no idea of. I didn't know what to do. Every day since she had been punished I thought to myself, "Should I tell? Should I keep it to myself? What should I do?" All that guilt was eating me alive! I couldn't take it anymore.

I watched her be punished for those horrific two weeks for my mistake. It was awful. But me being the good person that I am, I couldn't hide it anymore. I felt like all this guilt was eating me alive. Did that come so soon!? I tried bluffing my way through this dilemma. Did that last any longer?

Sure it did! Right after Nesha's punishment was over; I decided to speak up. About two or three days after her punishment was over I was in my room that morning. She and my other sister, Shahadah had gone to the store for my mother's coffee. While they were gone I thought to myself, "When they come back, no doubt I'm going to say something!" Is that so? They came back but Al' Nesha didn't seemed so thrilled when I shared the news.

When she came upstairs I said, "Nesha, um! Remember the time you were punished for scoring a forty on your quiz?"

"Yeah," is what she said in return.

"Well, remember you said none of your teachers gave you a forty?"

"Yeah," she mocked.

"You were right," as I spoke with fear.

"What?" She asked puzzled.

She stopped a moment and continued, "Wait! How do you know?" I then replied, "A few days after mommy grounded you; actually that Monday, Ms. Flores told me I got a forty on my quiz. I was shocked, too. Are you mad at me?"

"So you mean to tell me you knew that whole time and didn't say anything? Here comes mommy now. Go tell her!" She yelled.

"I was, I was going to tell her when the time was right. Besides she looks like she's in a mediocre mood today." I acknowledged.

I walked into the hallway before my mom could go back downstairs. She looked at me. I said, "Mommy, remember the time you thought Nesha got a forty on her quiz? That was me!"

She replied, "Look! We are not about to start failing now!"

That wasn't so bad was it? But if someone were to place that quiz in front of me now I'd ace it of course. But that taught me a lesson. I guess I really had to learn the hard way!

Charisma Lyles
15th Avenue School

## Smarter

Smarter is something we can all be
It's in our mind and our soul
It's the 100% effort you put in
It's in everything you do
But when you realize
Who it really is
The greatest person you can be is you!

Alexis Rivera
Ridge Street School


## Life Made Me Smarter

I was a little girl who knew nothing. But as the years went by, I became more and more intelligent. As I started to get older, I became more mature and a stronger more respectful little girl. Now, I am in the 7th grade. And yes, I have made many mistakes. But that's not what life is about. It's about making mistakes and learning from them. Life has taught me to respect myself as a young lady and to be SMARTER:

L – Learn. I've learned from my mistakes.
I – Intelligent. I have to be intelligent to succeed.
F – Friends. I have many friends.
E – Enjoy. I will enjoy my life.

M – Mistakes. There have been many mistakes.
A – Associates. Although I have friends, I have associates too.
D – Deserve. I deserve what I get.
E – Excitement. There is a lot of excitement going on in my life.

M – Me. All I need is me, myself, and I.
E – Entertain. I can entertain myself throughout my life.

S – Short. Life is short. So enjoy it.
M – Make a difference. Only I can make a difference in my life.
A – Active. I'm very active.
R – Responsibility. I have a responsibility.
T – Today. Today is a new day.
E – Everything. Everything counts.
R – Respect. To succeed in life, I have to respect myself.

Kayla-Lee Zayas
McKinley School

## Smarter In Math Facts

So, here is my best method for use. The only thing you have to remember is that they are all family. Just do it step by step, step by step and I guarantee you will get it in time. If you are not a fast learner, you know what, that is not as bad because you'll still get it. You may get it in a day. Some people get it in a day; some people may get it in two months. It doesn't mean you're not smart. But just remember that if you don't get it, it doesn't mean that you are not smart. You still have more time. It took me at least a month and a half to get to algebra and everything. So I am telling you now, don't let anybody tell you that you are not smart because guess what? When you get to know it you get to shove it right back in their face. So if hey don't believe in you, well you believe in yourself. I am telling you, it's going to come. The light bulb is going to come on, trust me. Just remember they are all family and math isn't that hard if you think about it because if they are cousins they will help each other out for you. So there you go.

Quiana Bryant
13th Avenue School

Teliah Warren, Miller Street Academy

# How Do I Get Smarter?

As a student in the Newark Public School System, I understand that being smart is very important. I believe that I am a bright student. I have focused on my school work this year so that I can get good grades. I am going to spend more time reading books outside of the classroom. Reading is very rewarding. Sometimes I do not feel like reading which is not good. I learn so much when I read books. We learn new words from reading novels. My teacher gives us vocabulary words to look up in the dictionary. We usually study the words at home.

I feel that I am growing smarter everyday. I do my homework before I go outside to play with my friends. When I am at home I study my homework. Usually we ask questions and I like to receive tickets for answering questions, which proves that I am getting smarter.

Aneesah Carson
13th Avenue School

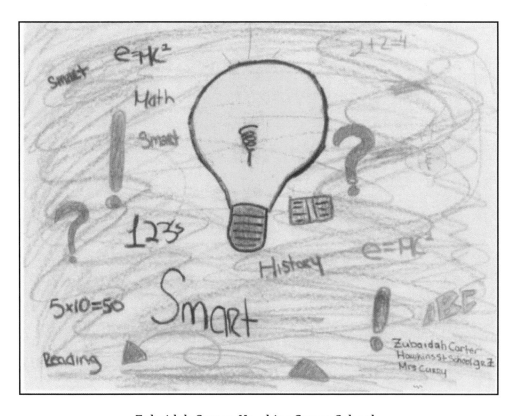

Zubaidah Carter, Hawkins Street School

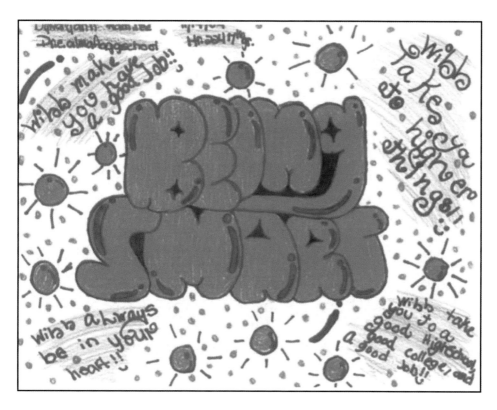

Maryann Ramirez, Dr. E. Alma Flagg School

## What Is Smart?

I think this means to believe in my dreams so I can accomplish them. I need to try my hardest when I practice on my *SMART* dream, which is dancing. I'm certain that I can dance, but I need to practice to be the best.
You see?
I am smart.
I believe in my dream, so I will achieve.

Carmen Melendez
Hawkins Street School

Guilherme Ramos, Hawkins Street School

*Stay Safe*

Jordan
Diaz

Dr.
William
H.
Horton
School

Stevenson Nurse, Miller Street School

## Smarter

**S** – Smart to stay in school

    **M** – Make it on time to school

        **A** – Apple for the teacher

            **R** – Reading books

                **T** – Teachers teach

                    **E** – Education is important

                        **R** – Responsible choices

Dwight Peebles
Avon Avenue School

# ACHIEVE

Achieving is one of my goals. I believe that I have achieved in many ways. One way I am proud of myself is by looking at life a little more seriously. I used to play and laugh, and always joke around. Now, I take things a little serious. Instead of playing outside or staying on the computer like most teens, I read one hour a day when I get home. Instead of just hearing; now, I listen when teachers are talking about serious things. Most of my friends say I'm so smart. Instead of just saying *thank you* and keep moving, I give them advice on how they can be smarter: like reading and studying so they can achieve also. I don't want to be the one smart kid in my class or my social circle. I want everyone I hang around with to achieve also.

I want to...

A – Always
C – Concentrate
H – Hard on the things that are important to me
I – I want to achieve
E – Especially when doing something I love to the
V – Very fullest so no one can stop me
E – Ever!!!

Michaelah Valentine (writing and illustration), McKinley School

106

## Smarter is Something You Become

There is a family tradition that I admire. My family sews very well. I felt I was not smart enough to sew because I could not put the pieces of fabric together or even seem to sew the right stitches. It was very easy for my family members to do it right the first time. I loved sewing and seeing things created with fabric. I wanted to sew but the only problem was, I did not know how. I had to strive for it.

I read books so I did not feel bad about asking my family and other people the same questions all of the time. I had some inspiration from my teacher. After reading and practicing, I got better. Then I had enough courage to ask my family members who were really good to help me. I worked hard and got good results!  In turn, I was able to make gifts for my family. I sold some things so I had the privilege to make a little pocket change for myself also. The best part was that I grew even more closer with my grandmother than I ever thought I could be.

Never say you can't do anything because you can. Being smarter means to learn more and to do better at something, anything. The more you learn, the more you know, the smarter you will be. Smarter is something you become. I could even teach someone about sewing if they asked me. I am smarter about sewing just based on my efforts and determination. I am really proud of myself and that's something no one can take from me.

Shaylah White
Dayton Street School

Yojana Torres
Dr. William H. Horton School

# My Book Angel

It was a normal day for me, until I didn't listen to my instinct and go home. Instead I went to the mall. When I was there I saw this antique shop. I saw a book that looked interesting so I bought it. Too bad I did! When I brought the book home and opened it, it started talking to me. As soon as it started talking I freaked out and fell off my bed.

"Are you a person?" the book asked ME.

I answered yes in my freaked out voice. "Are you a book ," I asked?

"Yes and no," the book said. "I am an angel trapped in a book."

"An angel," I repeated.

"Yes my name is Dan. I am 14. What's your name?"

"My name is Samantha and I am 14 too. So how did you get trapped in there? "

"Someone cast a spell on me. Can you release me from this book?"

"How do I do that?" I asked. The book's pages started turning and writing started appearing.

"Here I'll say the first part," Dan said. "You do the second part. With the power of the moon..."

And Samantha said, "When you hear my voice release!"

Nothing happened at first until Dan shook the book and then light came from nowhere. I do not remember anything after that until the next morning. When I woke up he was staring down at me holding his wings. I yelled, startled at the sight of him so close by. "How are you here? I am awake now. I thought I was dreaming."

"You released me with your magic."

"My magic?" I repeated.

"Yes you are an angel just like me," he said. "The power is inside you. Use it to learn as much as you can."

That is how learning changed for me. My life is not dull any more. I am my own angel.

Karmin Burgos
Dr. E. Alma Flagg School

## My Advice

Get enough sleep because if you do not
You will be tired and you will fuss and cuss.
You should get your 8 or 9 hours each night
Take my advice.

Study everyday for an hour
This leads to good grades,
Good education and a good job.
They might skip you to another grade.
A future of success will be made.
Take my advice.

You should eat healthy food
And not junk food because it has lots of sugar,
Which does your brain no good
Take my advice.

You will be smart,
If you take my advice

Lionetta Poneys
Dr. E. Alma Flagg School

Christopher Sornza
Hawkins Street School

## How I Became Smarter in Basketball

The way I got smarter in basketball was by practicing with people that know how to play. One time I even practiced with Randy Foye. He's an NBA player for the Wizards (#15). He grew up in Newark and was a student at my school, Dr. E. Alma Flagg.

Randy showed me all the basics, like how to watch your opponent, how to handle the basketball, and how to work with your partner so you can get an assist.

I've also learned that when a player double dribbles the referee will blow the whistle because you are not supposed to double dribble. The other team will get the ball. Walking and carrying are just some of the things that a player should not do. A smart player knows the rules of the game.

When I get a basketball I go to the court and practice by myself, and sometimes I practice with my friends. One day we might get drafted to the NBA. That's why we learn about basketball.

Edwin Toledo
Dr. E. Alma Flagg School

# Dance Is Me

Do you spend your whole day dancing? Well it's all I do. I prance and I dance. When I'm walkin' down the block and hear my tunes you know I'm going to stop and show my moves!

I dance here and I dance over there, hey I dance everywhere!

I do all types of dance from hip-hop to jazz, to ballet and salsa.

'Cause dancing is me, and that's what I do! I live and love dance. I don't fear dance. I am dance. To me dance is that special thing that helps you. Dance teaches you things in its own special way.

Dance makes me smarter!

I learn different cultures and styles, I could survive world-wide. I learn different ways to move. Dance helps me understand different feelings and emotions. One day you should check it out cause it's really cool!

I'm just like dance with its big ego and swagger. When I'm performing in front of millions, you won't see me hiding. I'll be shining like a medallion.

Some people think dance is just *there* and that you don't learn from it. But you do. Just try it. You never know what will happen to you.

Llyasha Moore
Dr. E. Alma Flagg


# Becoming Smarter

Being smarter would be making the super honor roll
This would make my mom proud of me
Being smarter means not having to ask everyone
What is this or that-I find out by myself
Because
I pay attention in class.
Being smarter means knowing what is right and what is wrong,
Then choosing right
Being smarter means not messing up all the time.
People call me stupid now but as I become smarter
They will not any more.
My mom will no longer be disappointed.
Instead, she would be extremely proud.
I am surely working to be the smartest I can be.

Jahaira Mendoza
Dr. E. Alma Flagg

# I Love Football

I love football.
Football is the best sport, better than the rest.
When I play football it gets me heated.
My team is the best. We are undefeated.
I dream football. I live for football.
I play it for a very good reason.
All the other sports are almost the same,
But when you play football your head is going to be in the game.
My football teammates are killers.
If I play for the NFL, I want to play for the Steelers.
This sport makes me smarter because I follow the rules.
I also have good quarter back skills.
I choose the game plan
So there will always be an open man.
Because of that we never lose.
If you want me on your team give me a call.
I'll be there to play my favorite sport Football.

Marcus Nieves
Dr. E. Alma Flagg School

# What Gets on My Nerves

My brother Danny's mouth runs like a motor mouth and gets on my nerves. What gets me mad is that my brother doesn't listen to me when I try to help him with his homework. He wants to talk about video games instead of homework. How smart is that?  That is why he messes up on his math and literacy work.

When I tell my mom, she tells him to be quiet. But then he just goes in our room and starts talking. He thinks he is funny, but I don't think that it's funny that he wants to talk about video games instead of homework all the time. How does he expect to get smarter?

The only way I think I could stop Danny from constantly talking to me is to take him to my grandmother's home so *I* could get some quiet. She is alone and she has no one to talk to. Maybe his talking about video games will not get on *her* nerves.

Valeria Maldonado
Dr. William H. Horton School

## Becoming Smarter

**S** - School is the place that guides your success
**M** - Make mature friends, make mature choices
**A** - Ask questions in class
**R** - Realize that you must be reliable
**T** - Today and every day have tenacity and tolerance

In other words-be smart, think smart and act smart.

Jose Dominguez
Dr. E. Alma Flagg School

## What Could It Be?

A boy that made my heart jump up
With happiness every time my eyes see him it makes me run off to him.
What could it be, could it be his eyes that make my mind talk and ask
itself what do I see in him,
Or could it be his personality that makes me scream inside?
I have to find out what is so attracting me to him. Let's see…
Could it be his eyes that speak to me
That tell me that he feels something for me?
What could it be? Please answer what it could be?

I became smarter by writing poetry about boys instead of chasing boys
when I need to be studying!

Skarleth Menjivar
Dr. E. Alma Flagg School

**I AM SMARTER BECAUSE...**

I am smarter than you are because I read a lot
I am smarter than you are because you only think you are "hot"
But, sorry to tell you
You are really not
I may not get the boys, but I get better grades
You can keep the boys and I will keep the "A's"
In ten years I may see you driving those UPS trucks
While you'll see me making those "millionaire bucks."

Carmen Santiago
Dr. E. Alma Flagg School


### I Am

*I am proud and smart.*
*I wonder how much my mom loves me*
*I hear music playing in the shower.*
*I see my favorite singer walking on the ocean's shore*
*I want to be rich*
*I am proud and smart.*

*I pretend that I can sing.*
*I feel the love everywhere around me.*
*I touch everyone in the world.*
*I worry about my family being safe.*
*I cry about my big brother that passed away.*
*I am proud and smart.*

*I understand my mom loves me a lot.*
*I say I can sing.*
*I dream of being a singer.*
*I try to make everyone happy.*
*I hope all of my wishes come true.*
*I am proud and smart.*

Niasha Gonzalez
Hawkins Street School

## Get Smarter Rap

Oh yeah Oh yeah
Clap your hands everybody
Stomp your feet
Let me get right into my beat
If you want to be smarter
You got to go to school
Do not I say do not
Always try to be cool
No acting the fool
You want "A"s
You want "B"s
Whoa now no more "C"s
Just do good
Do not act all "hood"
Come to school
Learning is
Brain food
Do what's right
Do not fight
Everyone will know
You are smarter
Now I got to go
I am out
Good Bye

Quadir Syville
Dr. E. Alma Flagg School

## Have Courage

I remember my first crush
Every time I saw her I would blush
She was on my mind all the time
In my dreams she was always mine
When I stared into her eyes
A sudden stomach of butterflies

Trudging through the rocks
I stumble upon a letter I dropped
As I pick it up our eyes meet
Like the sun touching the horizon
My body quivers with fear
"Oh no, her portly brother is near!"

I think to myself
Nosy of him to ask
"What's going on here?"
Filled with nervousness
I start to bluff
"Nothing young man."

A nasty attitude confirms my suspicion
And also fills me with conviction
I continue my motivation
I block him out
Give her the letter
And see the smile
She is all mine

My first crush I will always remember
You have to have courage
In all stormy weather

Nicholas Cruz
Dr E Alma Flagg School

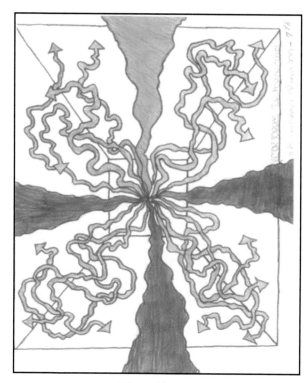

Victor Torres
Dr. William H. Horton School

115

# Ice Skating Smart

The time that I felt that I had done something pretty smart was when I decided to learn how to ice skate. I went with my friends. It was scary at first, that first day because I kept falling down on the ice. But, I knew that it would get better.

The next day, I went skating again. I was still nervous, but I was beginning to learn how to move on ice and how not to fall. On the third and fourth days, I skated all alone and practiced different kinds of turns. Wow, I can't believe I know how to ice skate after only four days in a row.

I learned something else, too. If I want to do something, I need to use my brain and make myself keep practicing.

Ouamaima Oumarir
Hawkins Street School

# Smarter Than Ever

My name is Jerrod Williams and I attend Miller Street Academy in Newark, New Jersey. My school is fun and I learn many things. In addition, I'm trying to get on Super Honor Roll so I can make myself proud. I am so smart and all I need to do is put my best effort towards all the assignments and projects. The subject I do extremely well is in writing. I love to write and I love my writing instructor. When I am in her presence, I show an attitude that no one has ever seen from me. Being positive is the best thing to do if you are smart.

To become even smarter than ever, I must pay attention in class and submit all assignments on time with quality responses. So far, I have gotten smarter in so many ways. I just can't believe it! I value my education now more than ever because I have learned that I am capable of being the head of my class and I can achieve anything as long as I believe. I attended a "non-Blue Ribbon School" but I know I am a "Blue Ribbon Student." When I achieve Super Honor Roll, I will know that I can do anything.

Jerrod Williams
Miller Street Academy

# Smart?

As I sat on that chair, in the middle row in the cafeteria, I saw it. My report card! I knew my grades; in a sense, doesn't everyone? Doesn't everyone know what they earned? However, I thought differently. I pondered an A in math because I'm great in it, B and C on reading and writing, followed by a B in social studies, and a B in science.

When I was a little girl and I lived with my father, he always said to us, my siblings, that he would take us to the movies. But the next day, he said that he couldn't, that he was not able to take us. This made me change my expectations. Now, instead of reaching for the stars, I reach for the sky. Along the years, I gave up and stopped trying so hard. Since I made my expectations so low, in a way I became low.

People have told me that I was smart, but I didn't believe them. I took my report card, and for a split second, I thought that I had all B's. Then, as I took out the card and opened it, I jumped! I got all A's! That's when I knew that I'm doing great.

It doesn't matter what other people say, even if it's your mother and father, your sisters or brothers, the only thing that matters is what you think of yourself. Calling myself intelligent is not going to make me any smarter; that is not the point. However, knowing that you don't know everything and that you can't try to learn everything but to work to the best of your ability is what makes you smarter.

This is what made me smarter.

Karen Montes
Miller Street Academy

Kia Thompson

Miller Street School

## Getting Smarter

**B**  Books
**E**  Experience
**I**  Intelligence
**N**  Natural Information
**G**  Grades

**S**  Social Studies
**M**  Marking All Subjects
**A**  All Grades are Good Grades
**R**  Reading
**T**  Teaching the Right Answers
**E**  Excel Your Knowledge
**R**  Reaching Your Goals

Ciara Gillette
McKinley School

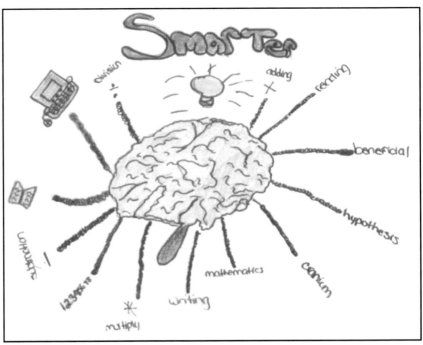

Diana Avecilias, Ridge Street School

118

# The Time I Did Something Intelligent

One time I won in a science fair. It started like this. Kids from fourth grade were having a competition using our science projects. I was so excited because first place was a trip to go camping. I wanted to win. I had never camped before. So, I went right home and got started on my project, which was about how tornadoes are formed.

We had one week to get everything together and make our projects. I worked as quickly as a cheetah running after its prey. It was so much fun. Everyone asked what I was doing for the Science Fair, but I didn't want to tell them. I wanted it to be a surprise and I didn't want anyone stealing my ideas. I was so sure that I would win first place in the Science Fair.

I never got frustrated while I was making my project even though other kids did. I was confident and happy with what I had done during that week. Science Fair day came, and everyone put their projects up. I was excited because everyone had the same things except for me. They had volcanoes erupting and global warming warnings, but mine was different. Mine was about forming tornadoes.

The judges entered the gymnasium to study the projects. My project was the last one they judged. So confident and so sure I was going to win. They were amazed with my project. I had two soda bottles and taped in the middle was the opening. When you shake it, the top soda went down to the bottom of the bottle. It went down in the form of a tornado. The judges loved it.

I received first place at the Science Fair and won the camping trip. My family and I had so much fun camping; it was the greatest trip I've ever had. My father and mother were very proud of me. I was proud too. This was my most intelligent moment.

Cruz Caldera
Hawkins Street School

Zahir
Hernandez

Dr. E. Alma
Flagg
School

## Smarter

Many ideas come to my mind when I think about what it means to be smarter. The first one is knowledge. When you learn things you get more knowledge. The more knowledge you get the smarter you are.

The second meaning for smarter to me is to have an understanding. If you don't understand something you won't learn anything. A person who is becoming smarter does work and studies. Once you have an understanding you realize new things. These new things allow you to become smarter.

The third thing you need to do to get smarter is ask questions. You will have more knowledge. Questions that you ask are important. These questions make you smarter because you are learning.

Finally, you should not guess to find an answer. You have to try hard. That is what smarter means to me.

Phaydra Holley
Mount Vernon School

## Be Smarter

Miss Baskerville helps me to become SMART by

Teaching me everything she knows

I can become SMARTER

I can become smarter by making good choices

I can become SMARTER

I can become smarter by NOT hanging out with the wrong crowd

I can become SMARTER

I can become smarter by paying attention in class and getting good grades

I can become SMARTER

Amber Morrison
Dr. William H. Horton School

**Shine Like A Star**

Smarter is something you want to become.

Unsmart is what you once were.

Smarter you can become with just one thought
A's and B's show you are smart.

Paint those words in your mind and heart.

Work hard and do your best.

Study for every test.

So let us all work hard,
do our best, and shine like stars.

Kimberly Morales
Dr. E. Alma Flagg School

**SPEED**

**S** = Scientists which we need

**P** = Planets which the scientists
discovered

**E** = Education which we need
to get smart

**E** = Eclipses are something
wonderful to see
(But not with your naked eye)

**D** = Density, the unit of volume

Karla Lopez
Dr. William H. Horton School

## Smart Robots

**S**     Smooth moving
**M**    My robot is so fast
**A**     Always has 100% efficiency
**R**     Reliable at all times
**T**     The best robot ever built

**R**     Racing around the building
**O**     OMG, that robot is amazing
**B**     Big, heavy machinery
**O**     Ooh, my robot is so great
**T**     The smartest one in the room
**S**     So cool and so smooth

Diamante Harrell
Hawkins Street School

## My Smart Poem

Is smart just a game that we play every day?
Is smart just fame in a sort of a way?

Are we smart because we are clever?
Are we smart because we cook chicken wings?
Are we smart because we can pull a lever?

How do we know when we are smart?
It's when we do something good
Or when we say something that no one understands.

We are smart when we walk
We are smart when we talk
We are smart when we eat
We are smart when we sleep

What is the lesson from this poem?
Every single person is smart in some special way.

Basil Thomas
Hawkins Street School

## Becoming Smarter

John, a pastry chef refuses to move to Mexico because he makes a lot of money in Miami. He tells his current boss Mike, "I have a high reputation in Miami."

Mike replies, "I understand but if you like your job you have to go to Mexico."

John walks out of his job mumbling to himself. "I don't have a lot of money to move now unless the company pays for the move."

After a restless night, John finally understands what would happen if he doesn't go. So the next morning he went to Mexico. Everything he had in Miami he got in Mexico.

John became smarter by learning everything doesn't go how you plan. Sometimes you get smarter by moving on.

I learned from John. High School is my next move. It is no longer so scary.

Daniel-John Gonzalez
Dr. E. Alma Flagg School


## My Fondest Memory

Our experiences can make us smarter. It was a bright and sunny morning. I was sweating with fear. My mom was taking me to Six Flags! It was my birthday and my older cousin was going too. I couldn't wait to go! There was one specific ride that I wanted to go on. It is called *King Da Ka*.

My cousin was so happy because she was going to go on it first. In the car, we began to sing a song we made up: *"we're going on the ride la di da!"*

Sadly, when we arrived the gates were closed. I was anxious to go in and couldn't wait to get on the rides. My cousin was so excited, she became super hyper. Finally the guy on the monitor said, "When the gates open free rides for everyone!" As soon as he said that the gates opened. Everyone ran as fast as they could. My family and I ran as fast as we could and we won the prize for riding every attraction in the park.

After we got on all the rides I felt so excited. Every time I got off one ride my hair was sticking up. My cousin laughed at me numerous times. We took lots of pictures to remember our adventure. At one point we went to a fast food stand and ordered cheese French fries, my favorite! As I ate one, I sneezed! Unfortunately, my cousin she received an unexpected gift from me on her face. It was so gross; however, the smart experience of learning the value of patience added more laughter to the most unforgettable day ever!

Sabrina Mendez
Rafael Hernandez School

## Look What Happened When I Listened to My Mom

I wanted to learn how to swim so I could swim by myself at the pool. My mother was teaching me how to swim, but I didn't know what to do. I always felt like I was drowning when I went in the water and tried to turn my head the right way so I could breathe.

I was ready to give up. Then my mother said, "If at first you don't succeed, try, try again." I did try again and soon started to swim. I am proud that I didn't give up. That was one of my smart moves. Now, I can swim by myself at the pool and not worry that I will drown.

Melissa Yanez
Hawkins Street School

## Smart, Caring and Curious

I am smart, caring, and curious
I wonder if the clouds are really soft
I hear the ocean swish
I see dolphins swim in clouds
I want everything to be free
I am smart, caring, and curious

I pretend to swim in the clouds with the dolphins
I feel the clouds splash in my face
I touch the dolphin's smooth skin
I worry about when the moment will be over
I cry when the clouds fade away and the dolphins leave
I am smart, caring and curious

I understand the dolphins need to be free
I say the clouds won't fully fade when the sun goes down
I dream about the dolphins and clouds every night
I'll try to be with them both one day
I hope I can fulfill my dreams
I am smart, caring, and curious

Tatyana Polite
Hawkins Street School

## S.M.A.R.T. (A Rap)

Smart! Making good decisions.
Smart! Coming to school on time.
Smart!  Being prepared for class.
Smart!  Being a leader.
Smart!  Staying in school.
Smart!  Getting your education.
Smart!  Following school rules.
Smart!  Staying focused.
Smart! Girls and boys is something you should do.
That is why I made this song for you.
Just to let you know, don't be dumb.

Be SMART! and stay in school.

Jewelle Dix
Newton Street School

Nashali Rivera
15th Avenue School

## Being SMART

**S** – Smart
**M** – Me
**A** – Achieve
**R** – Responsible
**T** – Talented

Being smart is not so easy
It takes practice to get to your goals
To achieve
To succeed
But you can't get there until you try
Study
Listen
Become smart now
It will change your ways
Your feelings
Your life
Don't give up.
Achieve

Natalie Rodriguez
McKinley School

**I'm a Smart Super Hero**

On Saturday, June 17, 2007, I saved my dog from getting hit by a car. I felt like a super hero on that day. A smart and brave super hero who saw Sandy Gillespie, my dog, run out into the street in front of an orange Mustang.

I yelled at her, "Sandy Diane Gillespie, get your tannish big self over here before I come after you." She ran back to me, and ever since then, she has never run out into the street.

QuyNay Gillespie
Hawkins Street School

Al-Mutokabbir Lawson
15th Avenue School

# I Am Smarter

To me, everyone is smart in their own way. It's just a matter of whether or not you like to show it. My story is like any other student's story at McKinley School: wanting to fit in. Children my age think it's cool to be below average. But, in reality, wouldn't you want to succeed?

I started off with C's and D's but because of my attitude and the crowd that I was hanging out with, I realized I needed a change. Now, I'm optimistic about my grades and proud of the way I achieved my goals. A's and B's are now my only expectations other than living any ordinary teenage life. Now I can honestly say that I have become...SMARTER!

S – Strategies are very important to becoming smarter
M – Mature is a big help to becoming smarter
A – Attitude
R – Respect yourself and others
T – Talented in your own way
E – Encourage yourself to push harder
R – Responsible for your own things

Michelle
Santiago
(writing and
illustration)
McKinley School

## How You Feel Inside

You fall down to get back up.
Again it seems like everyone has something to say.
This world wants to see you fall.
You fall down
You're spinning around
Never to see the light again.
You repeat the same words over and over again.
I've never seen you smile.
You're always looking down on me.
Look at me
and let me feel the pain that you feel.
I want to see life through your eyes.
There's no place inside,
The misery fills your veins.

Cristina Cartegena
Dr. William H. Horton School

Craig Jacobs, Dr. William H. Horton School

## Sticks and Stones

"Sticks and stones may hurt my bones, but words will never hurt me."

What this quote means to me is that, yes, sticks and stones may break your bones but that words will never overpower someone's feeling. I find this quote to be misleading. I've heard this quote many times before and I still disagree with it. I know that words can't hurt you physically, but they can definitely hurt someone mentally or emotionally. If someone says something that I find offensive to me I would sure be hurt mentally or emotionally.

Everyone gets offended at times, but they are mostly offended if it deals with offensive words. I know for a fact that at one point many people have been teased in their life. I know that I have, and I know that it really hurt my feelings so that is also a reason why I disagree with the quote. Not all words are offensive nor can they hurt someone's feelings it just depends on how the words are used and what they mean.

Words can really hurt someone emotionally. Let's say that you have a person that you really like, but then all of a sudden that person doesn't like you anymore; instead they say something that will really hurt you emotionally. You will be devastated and will have a broken heart. That will affect you emotionally. When it comes down to something that includes drama, it will always involve your emotions and that situation will affect you emotionally.

Pain is not only physical pain; there are different types of pain. The quote might be saying that words can't overpower a person's feelings but I have encountered and experienced many situations where I have been hurt and overpowered by words.

I emphatically disagree with this quote and that my beliefs are very different.

Jonathan Molina
Dr. William H. Horton School

# My Education, My Future

When I watched President Barack Obama speak about how important our education and future are, I was inspired. He spoke about how we are not to make excuses and to keep trying. He also said that you should not give up when things are tough. His exact words, "No one has written your destiny for you. Here in America, you write your own destiny. You make your own future." President Obama gave an example of himself as he grew up. He could not afford to go to school where most children went. So, his mom taught him extra things as early as 4:30 in the morning. However, his limited education did not stop him from being the President of the United States of America. President Obama also said, "I'm working hard to fix up your classrooms and get you the books, equipment and computers you need to learn. But, you have your part too."

I am going to do my part by completing all my homework and studying for tests. When I do my homework, I will make sure my answers make sense. I will ask for help when I need it. In addition, when I study for tests, I will not cram or study the day before. I will study each day, so I will be sure to excel like President Obama. As he stated, I will not let myself down or most importantly, let my country down.

Sumayah Medlin
Luis Muñoz Marin School

Angel Burgos
Miller Street School

## Smarter Is Something You Become

Smarter is something you become
Because
No one wants to be dumb.

You have to be willing
You have to have feeling
Because
Smarter is something you become

You always start out not knowing
But what you learn
Determines
Where you're going

You were once **unknowledged**
But now you're off to college
Because
You learned
Smarter is something you become.

Amaris Velez
McKinley School

Mē Lony Corbett
Dr. William H. Horton School

## What Does My Face Say to The World?

My face says to the world, I'm an honest, unique, trustworthy, and successful person. I think my face says all of these things because I have determination inside of me to go places in this world. In order to do this, I must go to high school and then to college.

From college I will begin to pursue my career as an actress in movies, commercials, TV shows and other things.

I'm talented and confident in myself and I have worked very hard to get where I am now, and where I will be in the near future.

If somebody tells you that you can't do something with your life, or you can't be somebody, don't listen to them. Pursue your dreams because your goals and dreams have no limit.

Yahzayah Bailey
Dr. William Horton School

## Barack: A Smart Man

**B**  Brain that solves world problems
**A**  Active father of two daughters
**R**  Really powerful leader
**A**  Academic lover of books
**C**  College professor and genius
**K**  Knowledgeable and curious world statesman

Bashir Herbert
Hawkins Street School

## The Hallway Was Silent

"The hallway was silent" there was nobody in sight. I looked around frightened by the dark. There was darkness everywhere I looked. Suddenly I got attacked by a man about 6' 8" with a beard.

"Sorry I have mistaken you for a zombie," he said in a deep voice.

"There are bad things out there," I said.

"Yes," he replied.

Then we sat in silence for a moment until we heard footsteps and ran. When we got out of the building we hid in a dumpster. The footsteps were still there so we hid under the trash. Next thing you know we fell through a trap door. We fell and fell till we passed out when we hit the floor.

"Where are we?" I said while coughing. The other man woke up and said the same thing: "I don't know. Where are we?" Suddenly, we heard typing. We walked through a hall and then into a room. We saw a man looking at security cameras and maps.

"I can't believe it," I whispered to the man.

"They are zombies," the man said.

We walked up to the man carefully.

"What are you doing here?" he asked.

We responded and he told us everything about the zombies and how they were made. He said we were going to go to an airport where his airplane was. When we got there we were to take his plane to South America where there was food and water. He said the people there were nice and not scary at all.

Lesson learned: You cannot be afraid of people and things you do not know. You have to keep an open mind. I am getting smarter because I use my mind to imagine great things and to grow more open minded. Writing also helps me relax and share my thoughts with others. I can explore things real and imagined.

Luis Villegas
Dr E. Alma Flagg School

Y'Annique Sousa
Dr. William H. Horton School

I got smarter by creating a story out of a song line and I have written it below:

# Get Out Alive

"Ahhh" said a military soldier in war; he has been shot. A soldier code named Dark Shadow passed by the wounded soldier.

"Soldier, come here. Listen and listen good because I'm only going to say this once. Don't leave not even one of the enemies alive. <u>Don't leave your life in someone else's hands, they're bound to steal it away. Don't hide your mistake cause they'll find you and burn you.</u>"

Those were his last words as he faded away slowly; then he died.

Dark Shadow ran away to the escape helicopter.

Lesson:
Sometimes you have to start moving and listening
at the same time to become smarter.

Mike Polanco
Dr. E. Alma Flagg School

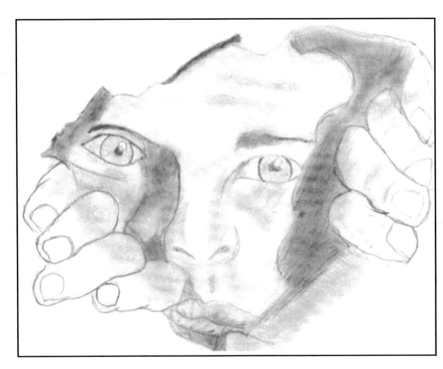

Kelvin Minier

Dr. William H. Horton School

# The Bird

One day a bird flew into our house. The whole family was at home at the time when the bird few in through an open window. Everyone was going crazy trying to hit the bird and send him back out the window. But he wouldn't fly back out the window. My mom and sister were really worried. He flew into every room of the house. After my sister's room, he flew into my room. My room is very big, and we could not reach him on the ceiling. He was in there for about an hour and a half. Everyone wanted to kill the bird. I thought to myself, "that would be a bad idea." They threw shoes and anything they could get their hands on. My father took the broom and tried to hit the bird with it but he missed and the bird flew down towards us. Everyone went crazy again.

I spoke up and said, "We can't kill this bird. It deserves to be free." So I did a loud whistle and amazingly, the bird came to me. He sat right on my shoulder and he stayed there. My family wanted to get him but I said, "No, I have to set him free." So I walked him to the open window slowly and he flew out. I showed bravery by standing up to my family and not letting them kill the bird. I felt good about setting the bird free because he probably had a family and he did not deserve to die.

Breyon Francis
Chancellor Avenue School

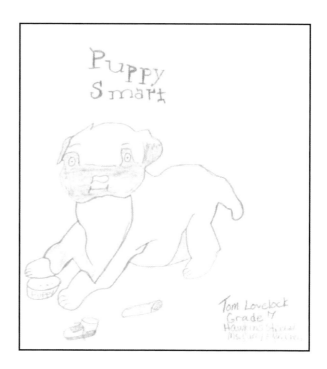

Tom Lovelock
Hawkins Street School

# Respect

My first day at Chancellor Avenue School was when I was in the sixth grade. My mom and dad took me to school and then they walked me to my class. I met my new teacher and classmates. At first I was shy and I cried for three days because everybody was talking about me and pointing at me, but then I got less shy because I made new best friends. They were Tytanisha and Rosa. My teacher, Ms. Morales, was kind of nice because she helped me with reading and spelling.

Respect means a lot to me. You should give everybody respect. If you give someone respect you don't curse at them, you don't push them, you don't talk over that person, and you don't talk behind that person's back. That is what respect means.

If I respect my classmates, I will get respect back. I have great respect for my teachers and my mom and dad. Now that I am in the seventh grade, I will respect my teacher and my classmates. I earn respect by listening to my teacher and studying hard to get good grades. I come to school every day. I am not being mean to other people.

I have a new best friend and her name is Jasmine. She goes to Camden Middle School. I met her in my neighborhood. She is from Africa. Meeting a girl who is from a different country is great because you can learn about her country. When I met her I said, "Welcome to America." I showed her around and we became good friends.

I knew Jasmine was African before she told me. She was dressed like we were, but she spoke "African." That's how I knew she was from a different continent. Jasmine's country is South Africa. Based on Jasmine and her family, I think African people are the nicest people I've ever met. When I saw Jasmine on my block and she did not meet anybody. She was lost. I helped her out because she did not know where she was going. After that, she told me where she was from and what her name was. Then after that we became best friends.

Katrina Amos
Chancellor Avenue School

# Anthony

I am a shy person who fools around sometimes, and I love dogs.

My friends brag. They say that I am funny to them. Also, my mother loves my personality. As a result, my family talks about me and says good things about me. The most significant thing that I do of value is helping others. Also, I stop polluting a lot. I take out the garbage. This is important to the world. It makes me feel good inside.

My goal is to play basketball. I want to pay for the Cleveland Cavaliers or the Denver Nuggets. I am going to be a champion. I am unique and special especially because I have a great goal to reach.

Anthony Levett
Chancellor Avenue School

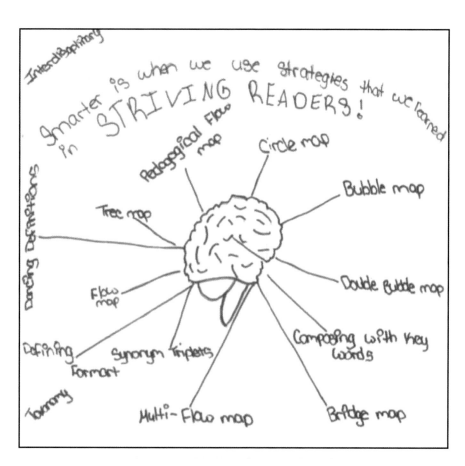

Daisja Polite, Ridge Street School

# Smarter: Grade 8 Contributors

## Little Big Planet

Once upon a time in little big planet there was a mighty sackboy. He was very strong and had all kinds of feelings—sad, annoyed, happy and scared. These adventures take sackboy on the king's adventures to capture the collector who has taken all of the creators ideas.

Now sackboy goes through many adventures and not just the king's adventures. He goes through the graveyard, Mexico, New York, China, India and many more places in search of the collector.

At the end it all comes down to it.

So, can you save little big planet?

Reinaldo Rivera
Rafael Hernandez School


## What Place Do You Think of When You Think of Total Darkness?

The place I think of is the world. This world is engulfed in darkness. It shrouds the light deep in our hearts. The pain is the darkness. All the anger, hate, racism, fear and death are in this world. People say this world is peaceful, but it is not. People (all people) need to understand that we have to enlighten ourselves with wisdom if we are to find peace.

War just brings senseless violence to people around the world. War is like playing God. Generals decide what area to destroy next. But I must respect the soldiers who give their lives and are in the army to protect families and generations to come.

We are all connected somehow by an invisible tie—our human love for each other. All life is sacred. It's important to protect it. If it is necessary to wipe out an evil for the sake of all life, I would stand with it.

Albin Fermin
Dr. William Horton School

**Smarter**

Smarter is what you can achieve
Smarter is something you can accomplish
Smarter is what you become.

Smarter is what you should want to be
Smarter should be a goal
Smarter is what you become

Smarter is an opportunity
Smarter is power you gain
Smarter is what you become.

Halimah Muhammad
Avon Avenue School


## Energy Transformation

Energy transformation is when energy changes its state. Since energy can neither be destroyed nor created, it has to change. The sun's solar energy is absorbed by the apple tree. Then the tree uses the rays of the sun to undergo photosynthesis. This is the process of using light to make glucose or sugar. Then a human eats one of the apples from the tree. Chemical energy then takes place when the apple is digested by the human. The energy from the apple then makes her active. She decides to play soccer. This leads to kinetic or moving energy. She moves around a lot when she kicks the ball. After her activeness, she feels exhausted. Her kinetic energy now turns to potential or stored energy as she rests.

Honoriah Wah
Chancellor Avenue School

Drawing:
Francielly Alvarez &
Ameerah Carson
Chancellor Avenue School

**Smarter Is Something You Become**

What this quote means to me is that you cannot be smarter,
You must become smarter.

Also that you can try and work hard and
Become smarter.

Moreover, whenever you think that you are smart,
Just know that you can get smarter,
If you try

Tyanna Smith
Avon Avenue School

Smarter

It's what you become

Being smart isn't given to you at birth

its earned and showed

throughout your whole life

By: Deandre Thomas
Avon Avenue School
Grade 8

**Smarter Is What I Am**

Smart is what I am.
Smart is something that starts with a "wham."
Smart is something that begins with an "S."
Smart is something that puts out the word best.
Smart is something you have won.
Smart is something you have become.
Smart is something you dream.
Smart is something you beam.
Smart is something you want.
Smart is something you admire.
Smart is something you succeed.
Smart is something you believe.
Smart is something you hear.
Smart is something you want.
Smart is something that makes you who you are.
Smart is something that reaches for you.
Smart is something I am.

Tynasia McKinney
Avon Avenue School


## Love

The heart wants what the heart wants
Love comes and goes when the heart wants
No one can stop the love
Love leads to mysterious places
A heart is dying in blood for its bait
Girls cannot get enough when the power of love is here
Romance, species, things heat up but never die out
Hearts pump thump and again
Thump! Pump!
How does the love come?
Smart? Smarter? Smartest?

Rachael Acevedo
Luis Muñoz Marin Middle School

## Friends or Traitors?

It was a day,
But no ordinary day
When something happened in a difficult way.
A person calls another person
Their best friend;
They promised the friendship would last forever,
But in my book it lasts, never.
When you finally trust them with all your might
Something hits you and becomes out of sight.
And then you realize they're not really your friend;
Not someone you can trust,
But a traitor that blows away like dust.

Leslie A. Soto
Rafael Hernandez School


## Poverty

Do you think someone would succeed in a poverty-infested community? Yes, I think one of the greatest challenges facing mankind today is poverty. To help I would give a lot back to the community by doing a lot of community service.

Gary Soto overcame poverty by forcing himself to work. He is famous for his writing even though his family was poor. Gary Soto serves as an example of a person who preserved and succeeded against all odds. Perseverance means not to quit. It's important because if you quit you are not going to succeed in life.

I persevere, that's what makes me a good student. I hardly miss any days of school or come to school late. I am very active; I love sports and participate in a lot of school activities. My goal is to become a detective. I choose to apply to Bloomfield Tech because that school has accomplished many things.

In my school I help with pep rallies. I am currently a Newark Police Enforcement Explorer. This program has helped me give back to the community, to be professional at all times, and it is also teaching me about law enforcement.

I plan to go to college then from there take my police test and work my way up to become a detective.

Pablo Morel
Rafael Hernandez School

## "If You Find a Path With No Obstacles, It Probably Doesn't Lead Anywhere"

What do you think this quote means to you? In my opinion, I feel like I can relate to this quote because it makes me think about the mistakes I have been through, when I start thinking about the part in the quote where it states, "without obstacles it probably doesn't lead anywhere." In other words, to me this is saying if you find the easy way out of things, you will never come out with what you want.

What this quote means to me is that you can never take the path with no ending. Some people choose to go through a wrong path, which isn't such a good idea; they also believe that the easy way out of things will bring you to an easier life. But in my opinion I believe it's better to face obstacles because you turn out with great results. This quote has two symbolic words, which are path and obstacles. They don't really mean find a path because it's like a road, but in this case it's a decision you will have to choose mentally in your life. There aren't really obstacles hitting you on your way through these decisions so it's also a symbolic word. What they mean is the ups and downs in your life that interrupt you in between your decisions.

In my life I was faced with many obstacles of all types, good and bad. I learned to get through them without facing back or giving up. I am proud of myself because I never gave up and I always tried. I have been faced with problems in my family and friends. When I was younger I went under peer pressure. I didn't know what to do. I felt like following and doing whatever my friends did was the best thing to do but I learned with my mistakes that it's not a good idea.

My aunt passed away when I was twelve years old. I still need her even though I'm growing up and starting to be a young adult. I miss being with her and her helping me with my problems and giving me a big push to do what I always wanted to do. She has left but she will always be with me, and help me.

In conclusion, this quote makes a lot of people start thinking about their mistakes and how they wish they could go back and fix it but the greatest thing to do is just face reality. What happened will always be there. It's like you're writing a book in pen, you can't erase your mistakes, but you can always do better in the end. It has given people a lot of advice not to give up and keep facing the world without backing down on anything.

Karol Dejesus
Rafael Hernandez School

## "If You Find a Path With No Obstacles, It Probably Doesn't Lead Anywhere"

The quote given above is a very powerful and thoughtful quote. It is very powerful because the meaning can help determine your life as you move on. It is a thoughtful quote because you really have to sit down and think about what you want in your life. You can determine this quote in many different ways; one is by the way you live your life. A path is like your life, you follow your choices as they move things you may not need out of the way. My path is to be as successful as possible, but with many different careers, as well as getting through the toughest obstacles. Haven't you been through obstacles yourself? I have and still do. Obstacles are the hardest things you come across and you try your best to get over them. What this quote means is your life without the hard things you try to get over to get better, is like not doing anything and not becoming successful.

This adage relates to my life because without my hard work and studying, I wouldn't be able to try to get into a good school like Science Park High School. This relates to the quote because it's a path with obstacles I need to get past. This relates to my life because if I watch TV and don't do my homework or study, I wouldn't be able to be accepted into any high school. So as I have explained, you see that I have had a lot of obstacles and have more to come.

This quote can make this world a better place by going through the obstacles that are needed. Global Warming could decrease if we make Earth a better place. We could help endangered animals. It could be the longest path with many obstacles but I'm sure we are able to help these animals. This relates to the quote by the problems that one issue can cause.

As you have just read, the adage "If you find a path with no obstacles, it probably doesn't lead anywhere" has many meanings and can be used for many issues that need to be solved.

Remember that a path is your life and you make it harder or easier.

Nalita Pillay
Rafael Hernandez School

# Attitudes and Altitudes

Do you believe the energy you radiate affects the outcome of your life? I have been asked to think about the significance in the adage, "Our attitude towards life determines life's altitude towards us."

After some consideration I believe this means that if you have a negative view on life and your mind is set to failure then that's what life is going to give you in return. Also I believe this means that if you are a person who gives up easily, life is going to do the same to you. Please continue to read my essay as I will provide further insight about my thinking.

To begin, I believe that this adage means if you're a negative person then negativity is gong to be in your life. I have seen this in my life by an experience of my cousin failing. For example, my cousin always had a negative view towards life and believed that her purpose in life was to fail and because of this negative mind life granted her this and let her fail.

Recent studies in 2008 clearly indicate that 25% of people who have their state of mind set to failure wind up actually becoming nothing in their lives. As you can see from the research how this pertains to my topic.

Moreover, I also believe that this adage means if you're a person to give up easily then that's what life is going to do to you in return. I recently heard Rihanna say that "Life's hard but it's up to you to make the best of it." In essence, this quote is important because life's always going to throw tough choices your way and it's up to you to make the best of it and not give up without a fight. Also because life is not going to be easy but if you try to take the easy way out then life's not going to give you a reward.

Additionally, in our world there are a lot of people trying to take the easy way out and they don't realize that by trying to take the easy way out they're just making it harder for themselves. I have seen people trying to do this in my everyday life and the outcome was always failure. Nevertheless, I know some people might say that your attitude doesn't affect your life. However, this is not always true because people who have a negative attitude in life always get chosen second and people who have a positive attitude always get chosen first. For this reason I suggest you shouldn't take the easy way out because you're just making it hard for yourself.

In conclusion, this is what I believe this adage means that people who have a negative mind come out with negative results and that if you're a person to give up easily then life's going to do the same.

A quote that also connects to this is the quote is, "Set your mind high not low." This connects because it talks about how you should have high standards for yourself and not low ones.

Alicia Teran
Rafael Hernandez School

Keearah Rushing, McKinley School

**Why Read a Book?**

Why should I read?
Why should I write?
Why should I think reading is all right?
Reading and writing and thinking would bring out the good in you.

Sometimes you may pick up a book and ask why should I read?
Let me tell you why you should read.

Reading is good.
Reading is fun.
Reading helps you write.
Reading helps you spell.
Reading, it's just so fun.
So, stop asking why read; just read for the fun.
And the smarter you will become.

Ty'Tiana Smith
Avon Avenue School

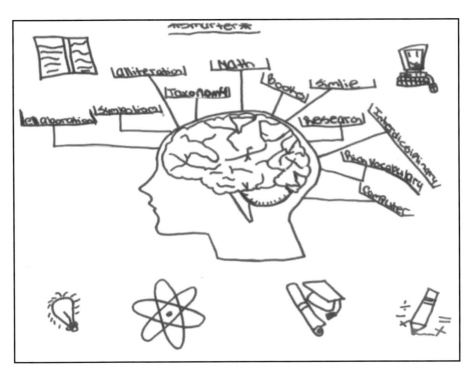

Karina Mora, Ridge Street School

## Smarter Is What You Become

Smarter is what you become
No one considers himself or herself as dumb
I love learning; you should too.
Getting smart is what you should do
Big, small, tiny, or tall
We learn to be the best of all
We learn each day in every way
If we pay attention, then it will be okay.
Having knowledge is the key to being successful
Try hard and you would have progress
**So you can be the one having all the success.**

Shaneyrah Thompson
Avon Avenue School

## "Smarter: It's Something You Become"

Do you know what smart means? Here's a hint, you have something to do with it. Still don't get it? Here, I'll give you a lift. When you learn, it makes you smart. Being smart is something everyone wants and something you want to take advantage of. Being smart gets you through the stages; the stages are: pre-k, kindergarten, elementary, middle school, high school, and college. You don't have to go through all of them to be smart, but, you have to have some type of knowledge.

In my opinion everyone in the universe should want to be smart. Me personally, sometimes I think that every time you learn something it's a way of you taking advantage of the world, it's like you are outsmarting the world. For example, if an eclipse comes and you know that it's coming, you can prepare yourself for it. This is an example of outsmarting the world.

Another way of saying you're smart is if you know a lot about a lot of things that others don't know and they ask you questions, you'll able to answer them with no problem. But did you know that being smart makes you who you are? It builds your personality and your personality makes you. So since smart is a part of your personality it helps make you, but it doesn't just make you, it makes others too. That's why "Smarter: It's Something You Become."

Delexus Greer
Avon Avenue School

## The Snare Drum

I love playing the snare drum
It's music to my ears
The snare drum is neat
When I play it, it makes me cheer
Playing the snare drum is my talent
It is my passion
I love to play musical beats
Both new and old fashioned
But I also learned to read certain notes
In the measures with 9 beats
I'm energetic when I learn new tunes
It really keeps me out of my seat
And practice makes perfect
If you want to be the best
So I go over what I learned
Hoping it'll turn out to be a success

Anthony Hunt
Bragaw Avenue School

# Dreams

There's imagination in your mind and head.

It's the land of your dreams when you go to bed.

You dream of a huge palace in the sky.

Where giant bunny rabbits know how to fly.

You dream of a twister spinning tables and chairs.

Or maybe having boxing matches with polar bears.

If there are monsters you can make them small.

By dreaming you're over 30 feet tall.

You can dance with a tiger and surf on moon beans.

You can do whatever you want in the land of your dreams.

Dayvon Burwell
Rafael Hernandez School

# Smarter

Smarter is something I will become
Smarter is what I can be
Smarter is what I strive for everyday
I am intelligent and smart
Smarter is what I am

Smarter is something you should want to be
It can change you and make you a better person
Smarter has many rewards
Smarter has many challenges
Smarter is what I am

Being smarter won't make a difference, unless
You challenge yourself to become smarter each day
Paying attention is what makes you smarter
Learning from other's mistakes makes you smarter
Smarter is hard work and determination and gives you a will to succeed!

Brianna Logan
Avon Avenue School

### Smarter

Being smart can mean anything.
Police Officers, Doctors, and Teachers.
It is important to be smart.
Knowing that you are smart.
Musicians, Tellers, and Authors.
It is brilliant to be smart.
Everyone is smart.
Celebrities, Models, and Actors.

Rahsaan Pickett
Avon Avenue School


### SMARTER,
### THE ONLY THING WE CAN GET

WHEN WE'RE IN SCHOOL
WE ONLY GET *SMARTER*
IT DOESN'T MATTER WHAT IT IS
IT ALWAYS GETS HARDER
I HEARD THERE ARE ONLY TWO EDUCATIONS
THAT IS SCHOOL SMART AND STREET SMART
BUT EITHER WAY, WE STILL GET *SMARTER*
FOR THERE IS A LOT FOR US TO MEET
BUT WHAT WILL WE LEARN
IF IT'S STREETS WE RELATE
WOULD YOU BE COOL?
THEN AGAIN YOU ALWAYS DEBATE
THINGS CAN HAPPEN
WHEN IT'S THE RIGHT TIME
YOU CAN THEN SHOW,
PERFORM AND YOU WILL SHINE
BUT IN ORDER TO DO THAT
YOU WILL HAVE SOMETHING TO SET
*SMARTER*
THE ONLY THING WE CAN GET

Joe-seph A. Rosa
Avon Avenue School

151

## Smarter: It's What You Become

One day, in my fourth period class, someone told me that smarter is what you become. I never knew what they meant by it but now I do. I am a girl who is smart and nice and loves to do her class work! Most of the time, when I'm done with all of my work, I talk a lot.

I really think that smarter is what you become. Someone who cares about me told me that the more I listen and take down notes in class and then go home and study, then the smarter I will become. Getting good grades and good test scores means that I am smarter.

Ahquillah McKinney
Avon Avenue School

## Sure about War?

Bang! Bang! are the sounds of guns. Boom! Boom! are the sounds of bombs flying from one territory to another. I believe that war is destruction, an unnecessary battle, a failure to communicate, and a cruel and bloody massacre. Imagine waking up in a battlefield of disgust and hatred. There is not even one area of serenity. There is violence and damage everywhere. Dead bodies surround you. The horrible scenery of a battlefield can leave you scarred forever. A war is a bloody massacre! Every day you wake up and every step you take, there is blood and gore, suffering and pain. This is a horrifying sight! Your best buddy could be laying beside you screaming and crying out because his or her life is on the line. But wait! You cannot help because your life may be on the line also and you may lie there hopelessly. In war, you are not just killing your enemies; you are killing people that are part of another person's life. A little son or daughter may be anxiously waiting to see their mother or father. They may not get a chance to see them because of the carelessness of war. When you are in war, you are not only fighting for your country, you are also fighting for your life. You may have all of the qualities of a soldier. You may be audacious, bold hearted, fearless, and have stability. But, your life is still on the line. Being qualified does not mean you can stop a bullet from coming towards you. It does not mean you can stop the bomb aimed at your territory. You are taking a risk and trying to be a survivor. At any second, minute, hour, or day, your life can be taken away just like that. Think! Just think for a second. Think about the battlefield filled with gushing blood. Think about the woman or man that is taken away from a family. Think of stepping foot into that territory where your life is on the line. Communication is what a war lacks. Can we just talk it out? Put those guns down. Throw those mines away.

Briana Hardy
Luis Muñoz Marin School

## Smart Is Something That You Become

There is something I noticed after years of school
That being smart isn't different, it's really cool.

Smart is not a number or neither a sum.
Smart is something that you become.

I know it's in you, right there in your heart
Everyone in the world has to be smart.

You can be tall or short, you can be fat,
And at the end of the day, I hope you like my rap.

Just sit back relax and listen to your heart
You will always have a chance at becoming smart.

Smart is something you become
If you work hard you will be the one.

If you play all day,
You will not learn your work the right way.

All those years of school were cool,
But college is the one that rules.

Kids say you are stupid, kids say you are dumb,
But always remember, smart is something you become.

Laquan Davis
Avon Avenue School


## The Point Where People Want To Do Better

The point where people want to do better is when they are tired of being put down and may get upset for not knowing how to read and write. I can probably help you with understanding it.

I know you may not know what to do. One thing you are supposed to do is your work and ask a person to help you. Don't be embarrassed about what you don't know. I tell everyone that you should get a book and write in it each and every day.

Remember, Smarter is Something You Become!

Iijhane T. Horace
Avon Avenue School

## Smarter

Smart is something you become.
But to become smart you have to pay attention to what your
teachers say.
By listening to what your parents say.
Also, learning from experience.
You might also learn from the streets.
Smart, that thing you become.
But to become smart you have to strive for it.
And show that you want to be smart.
There are slaves all over the world, who wish they could be smart.
Smart doesn't come to everyone.
But smart is that gift you have to achieve.

Denzel Bey
Avon Avenue School


## Where Will I Be on Graduation Day?

Where will I be on Graduation Day?

Somewhere I can play

or lay and think about this wonderful day.

And what do you say?

I just may do this on Graduation Day.

Because it will be a lovely day,

but no, I say.

Where will I be on Graduation Day?

Walking across the stage on that wonderful day.

Troy McCann
Chancellor Avenue School

## Smart Energy

One day after school my mother wanted to do my hair. She used *mechanical energy* because she put the plug into outlet. Then the electric current went through the cord and that is called *electrical energy*. When the electricity sucked in the air through the hair dryer, the vapor gives out heat. This is called *thermal energy*. All energy is Smart energy.

Melissa Battles
Chancellor Avenue School

## Energy Transformation Scenario

There was a skier who was on her lunch break. She had a bacon, egg, and cheese sandwich with a Snapple watermelon juice and a couple of hash browns from Dunkin Donuts. Eating and digesting this food caused *chemical* energy to take place. The skier is getting her energy from the chemical energy of the food she ate. The chemical energy of the food will be used as *potential* energy when the skier relaxes for a while, which is what she does next. Potential energy is the energy being stored when the skier isn't in motion. Then she gets her gear and begins to ski down the snowy hill really fast. This is kinetic energy because the energy is being used when the skier is in motion.

    To sum up, the energy phase goes from chemical energy where the skier is getting the energy that was converted from the food she ate to potential energy, where that chemical energy was stored when she wasn't in motion, and then to kinetic energy, where the potential energy was being used when the skier was in motion.

Rosslin Mensah-Boateng
Chancellor Avenue School

# Difficult Times

"Thayris!" shouted my mother, waking me up with a frightened face. I saw her run to the kitchen as I lay on the bed confused. She came running back pale white. She opened the window only to find out our house was on fire.

I started yelling out the window, coughing, out of breath. I was looking for people as I yelled but the wind kept bringing the smoke in my face, making my eyes burn. "HELP!" I cried. My mom didn't know what to do. I could feel her hands pushing me, trying to save me. And at that moment I blacked out. I don't remember how I got onto the second floor roof. I woke up with the fire fighter putting the oxygen mask on me. In desperation my brother jumped out of the window and landed on the roof I was on. Thousands of eyes looked at me frightened while they took my mother and I to the ambulance. It seemed like the whole world was there at that moment.

As soon as we got to the hospital they separated me and my mom. I still felt suffocated. I couldn't believe we were alive. Out of nowhere a lady came to my bed and somehow she knew that I lost my bird, Sunny in the fire. That's what hurt the most. She handed me the softest, cutest bear I had ever seen. In less than an hour almost my whole family was there. One of my aunts took me to the bathroom to clean up my face. When I looked at my face it was charcoal black; the smell of smoke was making me sick.

When I finally saw my mother, they were putting stitches in her head. She had the biggest gash ever; she yelled in pain. I must say, it was disturbing to look at. It was reddish and the skin looked like pages from about three pieces of skin were hanging. We both stayed in the hospital for three days. We went to live in my aunt's house for about three months or so. Then we went on to live in a great neighborhood. I have two birds and a dog now. Everything is great now, but I'll tell you something. I will never forget those minutes that felt like hours in that house. Never!

Thayris Cuevas
Rafael Hernandez School

## Being Smart Is What You Become

Being smart is what you become. Everyone is smart in his or her own way. Anybody can be good at something. I'm good at acting, reading, writing, and making people laugh. Another person can be good at singing and dancing. Everyone has a talent but that's how people become smart by reading and writing and learning things on their own.

Everybody is born with something they are good at. Smart is what you become and what you are which is "Smart" you just have to bring it out and believe in yourself and you can be "Smarter."

I'm smart because I always do my work. I do what I am supposed to do. That's why everyone is 'Smarter' and 'Smarter' is something you become!

Samyra Jackson
Avon Avenue School

## Smarter Is Something You Become

Smarter is something you become. Smarter is what I become everyday,
When I learn something new. Smarter is what I want to be.
If I become even smarter, then I can achieve my goals that I have
Planned. Some people consider themselves as stupid people
That can't learn anything. Well, I consider myself as a smart person that
Can learn every and any thing that I want to learn. If I just put
My mind to it. When someone calls me stupid, I correct them and say, "No, I
Am a smart person that tries to succeed and accomplish my
Goals and my dreams." I try to take my education real seriously, so I can be
What I want to be in the future. I will succeed in life, because I
Can be anything and everything that I would like to become in a few more
Years. I am smarter.

Zarriyah Hall
Avon Avenue School

### *Believe*

*Never give up;*

*Forget the naysayers.*

*Perseverance is the key to life.*

*If you believe you can achieve.*

*We say we want to be famous,*

*We say we want to be president,*

*But, action speaks louder than words.*

*If you believe you can achieve.*

*"To whom much is given much is required."*

*"If you dream it, you can do it."*

*Forget the harmony-hushers and dream crushers.*

*If you believe you can achieve.*

Brian Pirapakaran
Rafael Hernandez School


## Smarter Is Something You Become

In life you have certain goals. Most of the time your goals are to become somebody that is famous for doing something or famous period. Well, in order for you to achieve those goals, you have to be smart and the only way you can do that is if you become smarter. Have you ever heard of the phrase, "smarter is something you become"? Well, it's true, smarter is something you become. You can't just evolve into being smart; you have to push yourself in order to become smarter.

If you notice being smarter is like saying common sense, but when you become smarter your knowledge gains. Many people become smarter but they don't use their intelligence the right way. Some people make the wrong choices causing their intelligence to decrease. Remember, smarter is something you become, not something you evolve into.

Tarence Anderson
Avon Avenue School

### Smarter

Smarter is something you become
Also it's something you earn.
Smarter is something you can be
Smarter is me.

Becoming smarter is something well done.
Being smart is something fun.
Smarter is nothing bad.
Smarter can be found anywhere,
At home, outside, and in school.
Smarter is something you become.

Kaylin Alford
Avon Avenue School

### The Earth

*The Earth is very large,*
*But we are very small.*
*We may be small physically,*
*But we are big mentally.*
*We are bigger,*
*We are stronger.*
*We are so powerful;*
*We are the untouchables.*
*The Earth is big.*
*It is round,*
*It is great,*
*And it is our home.*

Nigere Quinones
Rafael Hernandez School

## What Is Smarter?

Smarter is what I am.
Smarter is what I become.
Smarter is what people expect from me.
Smarter is what we all need to be in order to achieve.
Smarter is something we all take for granted.
So my question sticks with me,
What is smarter?
Smarter is Something You Become!

Ayannah Jones
Avon Avenue School

## Life

Life is just a play,
We act it out each and every day,
Life is like a game,
It's in the hall of fame,
Life is full of options,
Also full of toppings.
Life is full of confusion,
But there is always more than one solution,
Life can sometimes be ignorant,
But the best when you are an infant,
Life is unfair,
You can always shed a tear,
Life is Life,
You only have one,
So live your life and have fun,
Life is a leading path,
Life is like a long road,
Keep going till you reach your goal,
This is life.

Ebony Burris
Luis Muñoz Marin School

Dear Editor,

Imagine yourself in my shoes as an eighth grade student, or maybe even a new student at your school. I'm walking down the hall and I see kids getting checked. Suddenly, I see all different types of weapons thrown out. That can be really scary and encourage kids to transfer, with thoughts that it is a very bad school. Or it can be a good thing and make kids feel relief and safer. In my opinion, safety is the best way to go.

My first reaction I think that they should check kids is for their own safety. I think this is a good reason because everyone in the community is always arguing about non-violence in our community, so I think this can be a great start. Children should not walk outside and be scared to even go to school. School is a place where you shouldn't even think about not being safe. School is mainly here for the students' education, not for students to be afraid of coming.

Secondly, it keeps illegal weapons out of the schools. I agree with this statement because I don't feel there should be any reason why you should bring a weapon to school. Schools are not meant for weapons. I understand how people might want to protect themselves, but there are lots of ways to avoid fighting and violence. A good way is to start non-violence programs in school. I think students do this because of peer pressure, and then it becomes a habit. So I think schools break that habit starting with checking kids' bags and making them feel like they won't bring weapons anymore because eventually they won't like that rule and that would cause them to stop.

Lastly, why I think they should start this search is to encourage students to obey the rules and improve school communities. This would be another good reasons for starting non-violence because in this plan it includes teaching kids discipline. If these kids don't learn discipline, I don't think this plan will work out as well as if it included discipline. So discipline is one of the main parts to this rule.

In conclusion, this book bag search is a good idea for the kids' own safety, it keeps illegal weapons out of school, and it encourages students to obey rules and improve school communities.

So now you know how I feel, I hope you take it into consideration and agree to proceed with this rule.

Sincerely,

Amani Cunningham
Rafael Hernandez School

# What A Disaster

One day my mom and I were watching TV and we were having a great time. Suddenly the storm watch channel popped up and the announcer said that there was gong to be a terrible storm headed our way. My mom and I were startled. Next we decided to put blankets and rope in the basement. We needed the rope to tie us down to the metal poles that were in the basement. We needed the blankets to keep us warm during the storm. Finally we went to the basement and sat for about 10 to 15 minutes.

After those few minutes we began to hear roaring thunder sounds and screeching winds to about 60 mph. I was terrified. Soon I began to smell something burning. As I got up a loud thunder noise frightened me and I jumped with fear. I approached the window and looked out. I couldn't believe my eyes. I saw a humongous telephone wire about five to six feet away from the window. I screamed. I ran and leaped into my mom's arms so fast she could have sworn my feet were on fire. She hugged me with force saying it was going to be alright. Next we heard an enormous boom upstairs. It sounded as if something crashed through our living room window and smashed through our wall that divides the living room from the kitchen. I began to cry from fear. I was so afraid that I thought I wet my pants. Twenty minutes had gone by and the roaring of the thunder and the screeching of the winds ceased. I sighed with relief.

My mom and I walked back up the stairs and approached the door with caution. My mom slowly put her hand on the knob and began to twist. As we walked into the living room we saw that our living room window was broken, and the wall that divides the living room from the kitchen had a huge, gapping hole in it. We walked into the kitchen and saw a car door lying on the floor.

Suddenly I fell. My mom began to tap me and start to call my name. Her voice got louder as my eyes opened slowly. My mom was telling me that I needed to wake up or I was going to be late for school. When I got out of my bed, I walked into the kitchen and saw that there was no huge, gapping hole in the wall. I smiled and sat down to eat my breakfast. It was going to be a great day.

Eric Yancey
Rafael Hernandez School

### Rap

*It's hard to survive in the hood, when you are
getting put down, chewed up, and you're messed up.*

*I've been living in the hood since I was two years
old. I been in the hood through the hot through the cold.*

*This is where you toughen up, you can't let the hood
get to your head, you have to overcome the violence
and get your ed.*

*I am an adopted child; I had to overcome the
gunshots, violence, gang and the wild.*

*I'm going to continue to do me, get good grades,
behave, and be brave.*

Onel Gonzalez
Rafael Hernandez School


### Running

I am running
three laps around the field.
I am running from bears clawing a hundred yards
with the sweat freezing on my face
I am running for a touchdown
with sweat rolling in my eye blinding me
I am getting my equipment ready
on a Saturday
I am waking up at nine
to go to practice.

Jawan Alston
Chancellor Avenue School

# Smart Cell Phone

Hello, new world! Fresh out of the store! Boost Mobile i425 is my brand name but my owner calls me Fine Z-Bo. He also tells me that I get all of the breezies.

I am a white and black-coated phone. My owner is a right-handed man. He does everything with his right hand, as well as holds me with it.

Ohhh!!! And when he plugs into that charger, I get all happy and crazy charged with power! I feel like I can call the whole wide world! I have worldwide service, so I can call my family.

Another thing I would like to say about myself is that I am a very diligent white and black phone. I can do very cool things like become a walkie-talkie or call long distance. Also, I have web browsing. Surfing the web for new ring tones is what I do! Doing really cool things is what my right-hand man likes.

The thing I like most about myself is the really cool games that I can play. Watch me surf the web for other new games!

Now something I don't like is when my owner drops me on my face. Why? I get all bruised up and I am a very good-looking phone! When I get dropped, I get a little less pretty looking.

Also, I don't like it when my owner tells me that his school said cell phones are to be banned from the school. Personally, I thought that was a bunch of rotten eggs!

Before my battery died, I said in my heart and soul, "I think that cell phones should not be banned!" Soon I cut off and said goodbye and shut off for sure.

Your devoted,
Boost Mobile i425

Clifton Johnson
Chancellor Avenue School


# Smarter

Smarter is me.
Smarter is what I will be.
All of my work can be finished.
One person will only finish it, and that will be me.
I will take the final test, ace it, and let my parents see,
That the smartest person is none other than me.
It can be me; it will be me.

Jerry Hayes
Avon Avenue School

## Smarter

The reason why people go to school is to learn and get smarter. I want to go to school to become smarter. Without teachers helping us, it is not worth going to school. Some people want to go on the wrong path, which leads them nowhere. The smarter thing to do is to go to school and get a good and free education.

The only way I could see myself be really smart is by studying and reading a lot. By reading a lot, I can learn about all types of things. I could learn about different places in the world, about things that are related to science and even math if I read. I think I could accomplish a lot by working hard in school every single day and when the report card comes in, my parents and I will be very proud.

Smarter: It's Something You Become!

Bevon Issac
Avon Avenue School

## Smarter

Let smartness become your faith.
It's like a goal that you will chase.
You can achieve if you put your mind to it.
Don't give up because I know you can do it.
Let smartness take over your life you don't have to fight.
Let smartness take over your faith.

Hyshawn Butler
Avon Avenue School

## Smarter

Smarter is me,
Smarter will be,
Being smart is like being like me.
You can get smart,
By staying in school,
But not standing on the corner,
Selling drugs trying to be cool.
So everybody who wants to get smarter,
Stay in school,
Not going up to teachers being all rude.

Jawan Perry
Avon Avenue School

# Rex

I remember the first time I got a dog. I did not know what to do, because I never had a dog before. My dad told me to take the dog for a walk, so I did. Then I went to get my friend named Nuk so that he could walk his dog, too. When he came out, my dog Rex was fighting Nuk's dog.

When I called my dog Rex, he did not stop. When the dogs stopped fighting I called Rex and he did not come. That's when my friend Nuk told me to get Rex trained so that he will listen to me. I didn't know that I could do that. When I went home I asked my dad if I could get the dog trained so that he would listen to me. My dad said, "Yeah."

So I went to the training school and signed up for every other day of the week at one o'clock. When Monday came I went at one o'clock. They showed me how to get Rex to listen to me. They showed me how to tell him to roll over and he did it!

Dashaun Simmons (writing and drawing)
Chancellor Avenue School

# The Déjà Vu Times

Everyday I wake up and sometimes it's the same, and every moment always seems strange. I can't understand why my life repeats over for nothing. Maybe there is a sign trying to tell me something. During the day things happen for a reason; like trying to help my mother just to please her. I get scared or excited when I have the déjà vu times. But that doesn't stop me from having a good or great time.

I can see almost everything from my past. I guess it's trying to tell me that my future will be a blast. Life for me is like repeating myself from a child to a grown up. It's not very awesome to have this kind of issue. But I use this for my issues. The difference between normal life and déjà vu is the same difference in being a human being and a super hero. Having déjà vu is nothing like being a déjà vu. These are the moment of me having the déjà vu times.

Jasmine Younger
Rafael Hernandez School

### Smarter: It's Something You Become

Smarter, Smarter
It's something you become
Smarter, Smarter
Stay in school
Smarter, Smarter
Do what is right
Smarter, Smarter
You can do it
Smarter, Smarter
Do your best
Smarter, Smarter
It's something you become

Ronnay Plush-Williams
Dayton Street School


### Smarter: It's Something You Become

Getting up for school with **no problem**
Doing all your work with **no problem**
Because
Smarter: It's something you become.
Following rules and being confident with **no problem**
Determine to get a college degree with **no problem**
Because
Smarter: it's something you become.

Mecca Burks
Dayton Street School

## Smarter: It's Something You Become

You turn a day older everyday
With that you gain knowledge.
You learn to make wiser choices as we make mistakes in life.
We think about our choices as we go through life,
wondering if they'll affect us.
After all, smarter is something you become.

Sheerise Mohammed
Dayton Street School

## Leaders

If I were a leader of everyone, I would help people with their problems. I would help them get their lives back on track—then they would want to be just like me. That's why I want to be a leader. You can get an award for being a leader.

But some leaders are bad, like gang leaders. They want to jump and kill people. I want to be the type of leader that people want to follow. I don't want to be a follower. I want to be a leader.

Timothy Tillman
Chancellor Avenue School

## Smarter Is Something I Am

Smarter is something I am
I hope you got this on cam
I am a smart girl whose name is Ciera
I am something that smarter has become
Hold up because I'm not done
I get straight A's
I hate when people say I'm dumb
But they are wrong because smarter is something I am
Smarter is what you make yourself
And it's something that you want to be
And achieve…

Ciera Banks
Avon Avenue School

### Smarter: It's Something You Become

Making wise choices and being determined in all that you do.
Smarter: It's something you become.
Being responsible, dependable and setting a good example.
Smarter: It's something you become.
By having integrity and thinking independently and standing for what is right.
Trust me, Smarter: It's something you will become…

Elaine Wilson
Dayton Street School


### *I'm From*

*I'm from an overcrowded house*
*That is always celebrating holidays.*
*I'm from a headache of noise*
*And a sore throat of yelling.*
*I'm from a long soothing bath,*
*To take all my anger away*
*I'm from long Saturday nights out,*
*To a long comfortable sleep*
*I'm from straining my brain*
*In order to receive an A.*
*I'm from teachers pushing you farther,*
*So you can be successful.*
*I'm from a world*
*With several commotions juggled into one brain.*

Sameerah Stewart
Burnet Street School

# War is Not a Game

Currently, there are many people enjoying life by playing war game. For example, "Call of Duty." While people are playing the video game, they do not think how painful it is watching people die during real war. They think war is a game as if you can hit the reset button in order to win again. While playing the game, they do not realize how many soldiers they would kill. They do not realize that by killing real soldiers, they are also killing families.

Are you one of the people that play war games? If so, do you think about the lives that you are taking away? Probably not. You see, people just kill others without feeling the sadness that soldiers go through. I have played war games. It's really not awful shooting or getting shot in the game. But in the real world, once you get shot to death, there is not coming back. There is not a reset button. Also in war there is no healing in two seconds after being shot. War is not a game.

There are many soldiers risking their lives. Because of war many soldiers come back home with missing limbs, syndromes, or some return in body bags. This is because we have chosen to solve problems instead of elaborating with others. Real war is very different from video games. You do not feel the pain they feel while their tears fall down the soldier's cheek.

Another event you don't see and hear in the game is the sound of a thousand warriors' shaking in armor. The smell of war is not present on video games. You may not experience those  facts, but real soldiers do. In video games, you do not watch your friend die. They may be fun for you to play, but it is really painful to live it.

For those who keep playing war video games, you have no idea what the experience is like in a real war. You have no clue what it takes for a real human being to stand in the middle of a war trying to survive. Ladies and Gentlemen, this is not Call of Duty... this is WAR!!!!

Roger Ordonez
Luis Muñoz Marin School

Gabriel Yaport
Dr. William H. Horton School

## Showtime Smart

I'm smart as A's, smart as B's, the only thing I don't get is C's and D's
Don't get me wrong, they're all right, but the better grades can be tight
Being smart is getting A's and B's, but ain't nobody as cool as me
I'm the smart one, give me the credit
I'm so good you got to call the medics, call the popo, give me that loco
The things I wear is the polos
My name is "Showtime"
"Showtime" smart they call me
"Showtime" because I see in the dark
Be that "Showtime" I'm the only one I'll be there at the rise of the sun
Talking about the sun, the sun does shine; let everyone be the one to get that sign.

Lexus Thomas
Avon Avenue School

Ibn
Stevens

Newton
Street
School

171

## Smarter: It's Something You Become

Smarter is something you become, not something that you do.
Smarter is something you strive to become in school.
Smarter is what you become after putting in the work.
Smarter is something you become after several years of education.
Smarter is something you become by choice not by chance.

Jiovanna Mount
Dayton Street School

Tyhiem Hall, Chancellor Avenue School

# Dancing

Don't you love to move your body? Well I do. It's fun to dance to the beat of music. It's like an inspiration to me. Have you ever seen the hit television show: Dancing with the Stars? Especially the way the dancers conduct themselves. They get in the middle of the floor and show the judges what they are really made of. They get smarter and smarter each week with new dances and routines.

I started to dance because I realized it's really fun and I learned how to dance by watching other kids. Like those dancers we see on TV, I have to practice and practice and get smarter at dancing so that one day I can get in the middle of the floor and show the judges what *I* am really made of!

Keiana Williams
Bragaw Avenue School

## Smarter: It's Something You Become

**Smarter: it's something you become**
when you show persistence and are determined in all situations.

**Smarter: it's something you become**
when you follow rules and laws.

**Smarter: it's something you become**
when you set goals and work to achieve them.

**Smarter: it's something you become**
when you're making wise choices.

**Smarter: it's something you become**
when you listen to adults and peers to learn what they know.

Roberto Vasquez
Dayton Street School

## A Rap

Practice, practice is what you got to do
Practice, practice makes it good for you
In activities and all kinds of sports
Learn from your coach and practice what you're taught
Practice, practice what you got to do
Practice, practice makes it good for you
Staying in shape, makes it great
Learning your plays you'll go a long way
Practice, practice everyday, you'll get a lot better
You'll learn how to play in any weather
Practice, practice is what you got to do
Singing, dancing, and football too.
Follow your dream and keep on trying
Practice, practice, and keep on flying.

Marsellas Moultrie
Bragaw Avenue School


## Be Smarter

To be smarter you have to work harder. If you want to be smarter you have to put the little things to the side. And don't let other people tell you what you can and can't do.

I think that smarter means that someone is working hard and trying to get their work done. They don't listen to what other people have to say about them because they are all about getting their work done.

I think that if more people would want to be smarter, more schools would become better, and more students would pass their grades. And if there was less playing and more studying, no one would have to go to summer school. Ever!!!!!!!

Khasheem S. Hammond
Avon Avenue School

## Writing Without Looking

One thing that I perfected is something I thought I would never be able to achieve. It's what I call "writing without looking." It's pretty amazing because not a lot of people know how to do it. Sometimes the words would just slide right off the page. When I first began writing or trying to write without looking, my work always began to mess up. I wrote like a three-year-old.

Writing without having to look is seriously a fun thing that takes place. You get a chance to see what's going on in your classroom. Also, you can try to listen to other people's conversations (only if those conversations are positives ones). Some people have to look back and forth trying to master it. I did!! I am going to do that most likely every time I write any type of essay.

Joshua Benson
Bragaw Avenue School

## Practice Makes Perfect

I used to struggle all the time and didn't understand why.

I didn't listen to my teacher and kept to myself.

One day I came out and started asked questions.

I realized my algorithm was all wrong…

I learned from my mistakes and started studying the right way!

I asked for assistance and help on the way.

And now I can finally say…

One thing I'm very good at

Is the subject of math!

It seems so easy all the time,

It's like a game I like to win,

But how come I'm so smart now?

Was it magic?

Was it overnight?

Or was it me?

Sachin Motiram
Bragaw Avenue School

**Smarter**

I am smart, but who wouldn't want to be smarter.
Smarter is better
In order for you to become smarter,
You'll have to be challenged.
Challenges are good.
Once you are done with one stage,
You grasp what you had to do to complete that stage.
Therefore you have just become smarter.
Everything you do,
And learn daily,
Makes you smarter.
Having some brains is nothing to be ashamed of.
Smarter is better.

Truly Smarter...

Ferima Ballo
Avon Avenue School

## What Does It Mean To Be Smart or To Become Smart?

What does it mean to be smart or to become smart? Do you have to study hard? Plant your nose into books every hour on the hour? Or is it just something you are born with? Being smart is absolutely <u>NONE</u> of these things. To me, everyone is smart in their very own way!

For example, my twin brother and I are very different. We are both what people call "book smart." He has more intelligence with technology and I have more intelligence with books and history. We both have issues in some areas. He isn't that serious about his work as opposed to me who is serious about everything that has to do with my work. Does that mean I am smarter than him? No way!

Being smart is all about knowledge, confidence, and empowerment. As long as you have those things you are smart. This doesn't mean that you have to be an Albert Einstein. Just be you and you will find the smartness that everyone has locked inside.

Shantell Hawthorne
Maple Avenue School

## Smarter

Smarter is something you are
Smarter is something you achieve
Smarter is something for your living
Smarter is somebody who cares
Smarter is somebody who studies
Smarter is a person who can believe
Smarter is a person who won't give up
Smarter is a person who never fails
Smarter is a person who never says no
Smarter is a person who puts their heart into everything they do
Smarter is somebody who you are
Smarter is somebody who I am
Smarter is somebody, and that's you!

Lavonte Brinkley
Avon Avenue School


## Designer Original

It was short, it was black, it was strapless and it inspired me to start designing dresses and skirts. As I began to study and practice by watching more fashion shows on television and also I continued to watch all the beautiful dresses on the Red Carpet.

Now I don't only love short and black dresses, I also love many colors. What got me to practice it more was I got a lot of color pencils and markers on Christmas. I also got a graphic book and I began to do it and now I can draw anything that comes to mind.

As I began to practice and get good at it, I started to hope that I will be able to attend Fashion Industry College in New York City. Also, it might even become a full-time job for me.

I hope I will become someone that means a lot to my family and the world. I could even be a role model. This is also what inspired me.

Keisha Anderson
Bragaw Avenue School

## Smarter

**S**  Smart as a teacher

**M**  Making better grades

**A**  Assignments completed

**R**  Reading books

**T**  Thinking intelligently

**E**  Education is important to me

**R**  Run to school on time

Kijana Fauntleroy
Avon Avenue School

Carlos DeLeon, Rafael Hernandez School

## Smarter

To get smarter, you have to work on your skills
Don't play during school fire drills

To get smarter, you could become anything
Do something in class but don't chew bubble gum

To get smarter, you have to work on your knowledge
Act like you're about to go to college

So get smarter and don't drop out of school
Because people say school is for chumps

Smarter: It's Something You Become!

Davon Knight
Avon Avenue School

## Getting Smarter

I started getting tired of just sitting in class looking at the walls and not understanding why I was getting the grade in math I constantly kept receiving. One day I told myself, "I'm going to pay attention for one second and if I don't understand what the teacher is teaching I'll go back to what I was doing before, which was studying the walls." I sat up in my chair confident that I still would be lost in the clouds, I looked over at the overhead screen and saw ¾ on one side and 24 was in the denominator on the opposite side. The teacher asked the class, "What number belongs in the numerator across from the 3?" I knew off the top of my head 4 times 6 equals 24. I also knew that when you are dealing with fractions, whatever you do to the bottom number you must do to the top number. With that information I knew since I multiplied 6 by the bottom number, I knew I had to multiply 6 by 3 which gave me 18. Once I received the answer I popped up my hand and the teacher called on me.

"Yes, Ashanta," she said surprised that I raised my hand.

"Eighteen belongs in the numerator," I responded very confidently.

"Yes, very good," she replied smiling, happy that I was confident and correct about the answer.

After that moment up to now, I always wanted to do great in all my classes to receive grades I knew I deserved. A lesson I learned was that you should never sell yourself short. You should always believe in yourself and be brave.

Ashanta Lawson
Bragaw Avenue School

## My Name is Kyle

My name is Kyle
Being smart is my style
While girls make me smile
I stop for a while
Smart is my game
I have all the fame
Sometimes I play the game
But most times I act insane and feel no pain
Being smarter is what I need to be
That's my goal, that's my plan, you'll see!

Kyle Gettys
Avon Avenue School

# Love is Blind

Love is blind

And it can overtake your mind

Sometimes love isn't always what you expected it to be like

Because sometimes there's one person in a relationship who's not truthful and breaks the other partner's heart, which makes them feel like a half of them just died.

Love is blind

And it's not fair that the best of us gets blinded by it

Do you think that all the people who get their hearts broken deserve it?

It is not fair that people treat each other the way they do
because "what goes around comes around" and it will come back to you.

But I know I'm going to find love someday.

And I'm young and smart: only 14, and I have a long time, but I'm willing to wait.

Tanaysia Washington
Hawthorne Avenue School


# Smarter:
## Something That You Become

Smarter is me
Smarter is something I can be
I will accomplish my goals and dreams.
If I believe, I will achieve
Being smarter is being like me
To show what I can be
I will achieve my goals and dreams
Just because smarter is in me
Smarter

Tamadg Smith
Avon Avenue School

**Make It**

Life is what you make it, don't wait
Just stand up and take it.
Take your soul, take your mind, take your feelings.
Take back everything
Someone stole from you.
Even if it's your courage or your pride.
Whatever was balled up inside.
Never leave it behind,
Now what's in your mind?
Stand up for what you think is right.
Not saying be a bully, think about it
Put your mind into it, be who you are!
Never think of failing, but succeeding.
Keep your head up and walk as far as you can.
Especially my young woman.
Being a young man or woman can be challenging.
But let confidence get you where you want to go.
Love yourself first, everyone might love you too.
Respect yourself, everyone might respect you too.

Quote for each day: "You are who you are but can't be who you were expecting to be!"

Mytasia Dormevil
Hawthorne Avenue School

## Smarter

Smarter is something you can become. Smarter is me. The opposite of dumber is smarter. Life can be smart if you want it to be. Smarter can be anyone in the world. So let's be smarter and not dumb. So world, let's be smarter and don't act a fool in school. I want to be smarter and successful. People need to be smart and not to be cruel. Smarter can be our #1 rule and kids need to just stay in school. So kids, let smarter be our #1 thing to do. The definition of smart is someone with a good brain and smart kids need to do work and then when your friend is still in elementary school you will be graduating out of school.

Ayaad Jennings
Avon Avenue School

## Smarter:
## It's What You Become

Smart people are smart
And that's a fact
They have to go to college
To get the big pay checks
They are smart
And I am too
I grab all my books
Then head off to school
To get an education
It's all I want
If it's smarter you become
Then that's what I want!!!

Kevona McLean
Avon Avenue School


## Lost In Love

Lost in love
From the first time I saw you
I fell in love
When I looked into your eyes I was lost in love
When you asked me out, I couldn't help but say yes
As I got more lost in love, I couldn't find my way out
Once we broke up and you left out of my life
It hasn't been the same ever since
Once you asked me out again
I was lost once more...

Ayanna McKnight
Hawthorne Avenue School

## Smarter

Being smart is something good because if you are smart, you know a lot more than if you are not. Being smart is not something you are born with; you have to learn through subjects such as science, math, social studies, reading, and writing.

Being smart is something you would want to live with because you will need it to calculate your check or other things once you grow up.

Having an education is a very valuable thing to have because without an education you are going nowhere but rock bottom and the place you have to go after that is up!

Felix Santiago
Avon Avenue School


## Life as a Teenager

Don't expect not to receive consequences when you know you did something wrong. You have to stay strong and have strength in yourself to get you out of certain situations. You rather go through them than stay in them!!!

Fact: The top reason for teenage females to drop out of school early is due to teenage pregnancy. Twenty-five percent of females ages eleven through nineteen become pregnant and start to drop out of school. We are encouraging young people to be safe and make the right decisions.

You have to have strength because if you don't who else will.

It all starts with you.

Zhane Daughtridge
Hawthorne Avenue School


## Smarter

Smarter is something you are
Smarter is something you achieve
Smarter is something for your living
Smarter is someone who cares
Smarter is somebody who studies
Smarter is a person who can believe
Smarter is a person who won't give up
Smarter is a person who asks questions
Smarter people are creative.

Dasjavel Mcclendon
Avon Avenue School

# My Friend

My first time meeting someone different than me was when I was at a different school—the 15th Avenue School. We hadn't spoken much, but when we started getting very cool, we spoke and did homework together. Now he is my friend.

When we first met, he asked me what country I am from. I said, "I am American." He said, "I am Mexican." He asked me, "What neighborhood do you live in?" I said, "I live in one bad part of town. There are not many other cultures living in my neighborhood."

We became friends because we are alike. We like most of the same things. Some foods we like are chicken and patties. I like to go outside or maybe to the park. He said to me, "I like the same things." On Sundays, I like to stay in the house and he said he does that too. Some family things that I do are on Sundays. My family and I go to one of my brother's football games. Sometimes I like to play football; when I can and my friend will play with me. Some of the things that we have are also the same. I never knew that kids from different cultures could have so much fun!

Nafi Brown
Chancellor Avenue School


# Smarter

Smarter is something you become.

Smarter is something you are.

Smarter is something that you could be if you work hard.

Smarter is something you need to be.

Smarter is something that helps you pass all of your tests.

Smarter is something that gives you good report cards.

Smarter is something that gets you in the best high school.

Smarter is something that help you get in college.

Smarter is something that helps you get the best jobs.

Smarter is something that helps others.

Jasmine Stevenson
Avon Avenue School

## Smarter Is Something You Become

Smarter is something you become
Don't ever tell yourself you're dumb
Dumb isn't something you are
You can become a shining star
Stay in school and be smart
Therefore, you will not have to work at Pathmark
Pay attention and do you
In addition, you can do anything you want to do
Smarter is something you become
Don't ever tell yourself you're dumb

Akeem Owens
Avon Avenue School


## SMARTER

**S** – Spelman

**M** – Make Good Choices

**A** – Always Trying

**R** – Remember Each Rule

**T** – Tests Are Always Complete

**E** – Enter New Challenges

**R** – Great Success Returns

Shanna McCray
Avon Avenue School

## Smarter: How We Become?

How do we become smarter is what you say.
Reading and writing motivates you today.
How you become smarter like the other kind.
Just work hard and open your mind.
Smarter is better and what I am.
Get an education; this isn't a sham.
You can do better, study for a starter.
I made the changes and now I am smarter.
You can't do it? That's not true.
They can be smarter like me and like you!

Jarvis Meggett
Avon Avenue School


## Ridiculous Assumptions

Pushing something over the limit when it is already close to the edge is dangerous. I have noticed that some council people want to decide to raise entrance in order to participate in extracurricular activities from a C to a B. My position is to oppose this new policy. First, this policy is likely to endanger the health of many students. Second, students should not be deprived of enjoyment and entertainment (especially students who work extra hard). Last, adults say children need to be more active. So why make it harder for kids to enter sports programs? These are just some of the many reasons that I want to present. Can you bear the burden of mentally ill and stressed students? Well, get ready to, because if you adopt this policy, many students who are already near their limit, will overload causing problems and endangering their health. On the other hand, if you left things the way they were, you would not have these issues. Imagine if it were your fault that many kids live dull, barren and empty lives like the inside of an abandoned house. By making it harder on kids to be entertained by playing soccer, and other activities, you are taking to joy away from a kid. Not letting children have this chance is not fair. America has already been the country billed obese. So why make it worse? Children are blamed for laziness and many are obese. How is making it harder for kids to play sports going to change that? Maybe if the policy was left to a grade of C, it could prevent obesity in the future, while providing a safe environment for kids to play in gym and school. Can people of the council see now? Endangering the health of students will not work. Taking away happy childhoods, will not work. Creating chances of more obesity will not help either.

Joseph Reyes
Luis Muñoz Marin School

## Smarter

I am the Essence of a new beginning
For some their middle and their ending
The thing I do is shut failures down
My intelligence is brave for a girl from out of town
I am a smart, brave, young lady
When people say I am dumb and ugly,
I say at least I am going to get a diploma and a degree, baby
My destiny I await
Anything I do I always debate
I am a genius, just count on it
I am a Spelman Student; I know I can do it
I am a smart, educated, focused, and brave young woman
who always wins
I am just smart; it is something I have become.

Precious Harris
Avon Avenue School

Ashley Olmo, Rafael Hernandez School

## Smarter Is Something You Become

Everyone knows me. Even though I hang out with whom some people consider the wrong crowd, I look deep within myself and yank out knowledge and common sense skills. I'm getting smarter everyday. Either it is book smart or street smart; they both will come in handy someday. If I do not learn something new everyday, I will probably need help because my brain is sure to decay. This is why I am creating this rap. I'm getting smarter everyday, but no one sees it; guess what? I can feel it, believe me.

Smarter is something you become. If you do not stay in school, you might just be a bum. I am very smart, but it did not happen overnight. I could prove you wrong, even if you are right. I will lend you some steps of being smart. If I were you, I would listen because this is coming from the heart.

Smarter is something you become. If you do not stay in school, you might just be a bum. (2x)

Being smart is cool but smarter is the guaranteed opposite of being a fool. You have to learn something new every day. You know something that will make you feel super gay. Come on man you have to do your best, so that you can be the valedictorian, which means above the rest.

Smarter is something you become. If you do not stay in school, you might just be a bum. (2x)

Just like Obama, "Yes, You Can!" Someday I will grow up and be just like, if not better than, that man. Listen up, use your tool. No woman wants a man who's going to be a fool.

Tyrrie Neal
Avon Avenue School


## Nahla

**N** – Never giving up

**A** – Always willing to learn

**H** – Happy to be here

**L** – Learning is a gift for life

**A** – Always striving to be the best

Nahla Conover
Avon Avenue School

# I Am Smarter

I am an independent, successful, achieving young lady.
I wonder what I can do to be the best at all of my goals.
I hear that my presence brings joy to other beings.
I see my beauty and my elegant ways giving me the look of poise and intelligence, seeing me as material for greatness.
I want the best for me, and more.
I am an icon and role model waiting to happen.
I pretend that my surroundings will not affect my dreams.
I feel like no one is by my side.
I touch the souls of the heartbroken.
I worry about the complications life will bring me.
I cry about the suffering people go through.
I am the perfect example of a successful young lady.
I understand the struggles of my peers.
I say things to mend the sorrow in broken hearts.
I dream that my singing career sets off.
I try to inspire people as my haters look upon me.
I hope my prayers will bless the lives of others, and that is what makes me smarter.

Eyonnie Stevens
Avon Avenue School

Cindy Anyaegbu
Hawthorne Avenue School

# How Did I Become Smart?

Hmmm... that's a very good question. But in my opinion I don't think that anyone can become smart. I think that sometimes people don't always show how smart they are. Sometimes we let others hold us back and we can only go to certain limits when we are in situations like this. I wasn't always as "smart" as I am now. Sometimes I had times when I didn't always let my light shine as bright as it could have because I had so many other distractions. But as I got older I began to mature. With that maturity came a higher level of "smarts". But at the same time, if I don't actually try to show smarts or at least put forth my best then I will come up as less than what I actually am or what I actually know.

Sometimes even one's surroundings can affect their output. For example, when you take a student that needs a lot of help and you put them into a classroom with students that don't need as much help, they are bound to begin to get on the same path as all the others. I think that when you do that you really are exploring your inner "smarts." But me as an individual, I don't think anyone should classify us with the word special education or inclusion. I think that we are all equal.

Do some of us need more? Of course. Not everyone is alike. But we shouldn't be separated like that. Why? Some may want to know. Because everyone has something that another person does not know or understand to offer. So, in other words, if one does not have something another may be able to offer, then you have two different people learning two different things. So, if anyone is to ever come up to me, and ask me the question "How did I get smart?" My reply would be as simple as "I didn't become smart. I have always been smart. I just had to show it and do it in my best way."

Amber Brumfield
Maple Avenue School

### Tamara Paul

January 10, 1996, Tamara Paul is born
Smarter is something you become

February 1997, Tamara's first steps
Smarter is something you become

June 26, 2001, I graduated from kindergarten
Learning my ABC's counting 1,2,3, moving onto bigger things
Smarter is something you become

With wisdom and knowledge brings joys and happiness
June 26, 2007, I graduated from elementary
Welcoming a new year of hard work and achievement
Smarter is something you become

December 2009, ready to go to high school
With new beginnings and challenges
I am an 8th grader in this world
Smarter is something I became.

Tamara Paul
Avon Avenue School

## SMARTER

Smarter is only something you can become, not something you can be

Smarter is like a challenge or like running a race

You probably stumble on a word or two but later on in life you will not because you became smarter

Becoming smarter is very important, it is very important because you would now know things that you did not before

Smarter is like a privilege because not everyone becomes smarter, some people fall off or lose focus because their minds might be on other negative things

Smarter is something you win; smarter is something you become

Smart is what I am, and smarter is what I will always be!!

Donna Barber
Avon Avenue School

# Joshua

I am Puerto Rican and I live in New Jersey with my brothers and sisters. We all live in the same house with our mother. We have a father too. I study every day to make my daddy happy. I live in a bad part of town. My neighborhood is named Johnson Avenue. It is a very bad neighborhood because someone is always shooting. I'm Puerto Rican, but Dominicans live in my neighborhood too. I am cool friends with them. We party together on Fridays.

There are other cultures in my neighborhood. There are Dominicans, Puerto Ricans, and African Americans. I like to play football with all the cultures in my neighborhood, all the time. The African Americans like to eat pizza and the Dominicans love to eat rice like the Puerto Ricans. Just like other cultures, my family comes over to my house. Every Sunday, we all see football. Every Friday we have cookouts. That's why I love my family and the cultures in my neighborhood.

The first time I met someone close and very different to me was Antwan. He is African-American. When I came to Chancellor Avenue School, he became my best friend. We were in the same class but we met at gym. I met Antwan when I was in the seventh grade. When my best friend Antwan and I met at school we would walk home together. He likes board games and I like videogames. Antwan and I like to play football with friends. Antwan likes rap and pop music. I like hip hop and rock music.

I thought that Americans were mean to Puerto Ricans. For example, I saw this show about African Americans and they were talking bad about Puerto Ricans. So that is why I thought that Americans were like that.

We read about the Taino Indians last week in school. When the Taino Indians met Christopher Columbus on the Caribbean Sea, the Tainos lived close to the water near the beach. When Christopher Columbus' people met the Taino Indians, they had three boats. At first the groups became friends after thinking that each other were strange creatures. I thought that African Americans were not nice to Puerto Ricans. But my friend Antwan likes Puerto Ricans. Antwan is a nice friend to me.

Joshua Valentin
Chancellor Avenue School

# Who Am I?

Who Am I? I am a person who believes he can do whatever he puts his mind to. I would like to be very successful in the future and have a decent job. When I think of who I am, I think of a person who has desire and a will to make it in the future. I am also a heavy metal fan. Most people think it is abnormal for an African-American kid to listen to Screamo. I chose this genre because I found rap music boring. The only thing that rappers have been rapping about is their money, cars, clothes, and the big homes they have. Nobody really cares about that; but fans are blinded by the beat. That is why some do not listen to the lyrics. In the lyrics of most heavy metal bands, the lyrics involve parts of their lives that were tragic and horrific. It is not that I make fun of their tragedies, it is the way they place the lyrics in their songs to sound good. I also like to be athletic because I want to stay out of trouble and off the streets. I do not want to be one of those kids that are dealing drugs and sleeping in the streets. I like to wrestle because my stepfather used to wrestle and won eighteen medals. I told him I was going to win twenty medals and make him proud. I do not want to be like a sixteen year old who was the captain of his high school football team. After he led his team into victory at the championships, he decided not to play the next year. When he was not doing anything at home, he began to go out more often. He then got caught up in gangs and joined the bloods. One night, he was loitering around the corner mini market. A rival gang came around the corner in a truck and opened fire. The sixteen year old, died after being shot six times. This is why being active is important.

I also like to write a lot. When my literacy teacher gives the class a writing assignment at home, I would usually fill up three pages including the back of pages. I get carried away with my ideas. I also like to study about history and want to go to American History High School. I want to know about what happened in the 1600s. I want to know what happened at the Boston Tea Party and how the first car came about. There is a lot of history in things and people should start noticing it.

These are things about me. I want to stand out from a crowd of people. I am a gray hair in a sea of black. I am a pen in a pencil drawer. I am Dejuan Daniels, and that is who I am.

DeJuan Daniels
Luis Muñoz Marin School

# Smarter: Adult Contributors

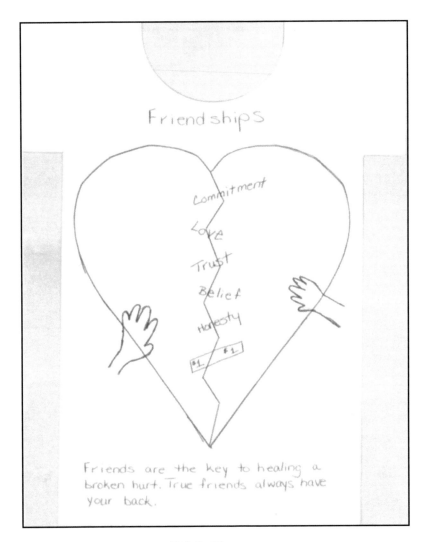

Friendships

Commitment
Love
Trust
Belief
Honesty

Friends are the key to healing a broken hurt. True friends always have your back.

Kakila Hunter,
McKinley School, Science Teacher

Feature Writer:

Matthew Lichten,
Ridge Street School

## THE POWER OF GROWTH MINDSET

William H. Johnson once said, "If it is to be, it is up to me." It is this belief that I had instilled in me by my parents when I was a child and the belief that I actively work to instill in my students each and every day. Having taught now for twelve years, I am honored and proud to be an educator in the inner city and I continue to set the bar high for all of my students. As a 7th grade teacher, I strive to promote a positive learning environment that builds on students' strengths, endorses personal responsibility and social awareness and taps into student's motivation. We are members of a diverse society, and students learn the importance of social justice and gain an appreciation for multiculturalism and diversity. My teaching philosophy encompasses understanding the interrelatedness of learning in context. In my view, in order for meaningful learning to occur, teaching must tap into students' motivations to learn by providing meaningful lessons that allow students to make connections between the lesson plans and their own lived experiences. This is supported by the concept of Growth Mindset – a concept that defines student achievement as boundless and positively influenced by self-efficacy, enthusiasm, and inspiration.

When I am in the classroom with my students, I teach them the importance of lifelong teaching and learning. I teach them that teaching and learning does not end in the classroom and that they have a personal responsibility to share with others the knowledge that they have acquired. I teach through strength building; encouraging students to succeed through motivation, effort and positive self-esteem. I believe that flexibility is essential and I meet each individual student where he or she is. I differentiate instruction by probing students with individually tailored reflective questioning that taps into metacognitive processes. Students are asked to not only critically engage in the lesson plan but also to critically reflect on their thinking and problem solving. I believe that teaching and learning are a collaborative process and my students are taught that Mr. Lichten will teach them but that they will also teach Mr. Lichten.

Another approach to my teaching philosophy that is consistent with the concept of Growth Mindset is that my lesson plans often incorporate an interdisciplinary approach to learning. I actively incorporate aspects from all subjects into my lesson plans to show students that the more connections you make, the more meaningful the content will be. To quote one of my current students, "Each discipline is like a piece of the puzzle, the more pieces you put together the clearer the picture." This resonated with me because it captured the essence of interdisciplinary learning and the importance of making connections across all areas of the curriculum.

I have had a wonderful journey as an educator in the inner city and continue to take pride in working with my students and their families. My students know that Mr. Lichten is a teacher that truly cares for them and for their well-being. I consider myself an advocate for my students as well as for their families and believe it is my responsibility to promote a rigorous and challenging learning environment that upholds high standards. I am grateful to have such supportive staff and administration at Ridge Street School whose best interests are in educating our children.

| | |
|---|---|
| S | Self-motivated |
| M' | Mindful |
| A | Awesome |
| R | Responsible |
| T | Thinker |

Ms. Lydia Curry & 7th grade & 6th grade
Hawkins Street School

# The More You Learn, the Smarter You Become

Laquisha said, "Ms. Haygood, there is no way I can accomplish this; I'm so slow and I feel so dumb."

I replied, "Of course in time you can do it, because smart isn't something you have; it's something you become."

Jaquetta complained, "Ms. Haygood, I can't possibly do all the problems; I can only do some."

I corrected, "You can learn to do all of them Jaquetta. Smart isn't something you are; it's something you become!"

Ebony's parent, Ms. Jackson said, "I have nothing to say at the PTA meeting; therefore I cannot come."

"Ms. Jackson, you have much to share. Smart is not what you have; smart is something you become!"

My student's parent worried, "Ms. Haygood, my kid doesn't have it, so to the streets she'll succumb."

"Not true," I declared, "She can choose judiciously because smart is not something you are; smart is something you become!"

Ms. Charity Haygood, Vice Principal
Chancellor Avenue School

# Model Explanatory Essay

Have you ever experienced obstacles? I think we all have. They are a path of life. I have been asked to consider the quote: "If you find a path with no obstacles, it probably doesn't lead anywhere."

In my opinion, this means that people should not take the easy way out of a situation because of what seems like the easy way out will really not move our lives forward. An obstacle-free life will not help us to grow as individuals. This quote relates to everyone, including me. The following paragraphs will provide further analysis of this quote.

I believe this quote means that if we have "no obstacles" or hardships, we will be taught no lessons. It is only when we do have obstacles that we must overcome problems and then we learn from them. I believe that is the reason all the stories and narratives have a conflict. That problem in the story makes the story both interesting and exciting. If there were no obstacles for the characters then the story would lead us nowhere and it would be extremely boring. However, when there is an interesting conflict, the characters learn a lesson and so does the audience. The lesson, also called the theme, is a result of the turning point in the story that only occurs after the conflict. An example of this can be found in the novel, *Number the Stars.* In the novel, the main character, Anne Marie, must be tremendously brave by tricking Nazi soldiers. She does this so that she can help her Jewish friends who are secretly trying to escape to safety. This was a difficult obstacle because if she got caught she would have been in grave danger. Still, she tries and succeeds in her mission to fool the Nazis and she delivers the package her friends so desperately need to escape. In return, Anne Marie earns a sense of pride for achieving her goal, and she learns that sometimes you have to fight fire with fire. By this I mean that given the Nazis' dishonesty and injustice, she knew that she would also have to behave the same as they did in order to beat the Nazis at their own game. As a result, the reader also learns a lesson about bravery and how everyone, no matter how young, has a positive contribution to make to society. My point is that no one would learn a lesson, whether in real life or in fictional narratives, unless there were obstacles to overcome.

To me this quote suggests that obstacles lead to the path of success but a lack of obstacles leads nowhere because nothing is gained. To further prove my point I would like to consider my own experiences with my friends and fellow movie goers. We often discuss whether or not we enjoyed a particular film and our reasons why we liked or did not like a movie. What I discovered is that a key component in determining whether a movie was good or not all hinges on the conflict and resolution. A conflict and its ultimate climax are important factors that determine our enjoyment of the movie. The more exciting and the more believable the obstacles faced by the characters, the more satisfied we are with the cinematic experience. I believe this means that we are best entertained when there is an appealing problem or crisis. I think the same is true in real life too. Both in reality and in fiction obstacles are necessary. As further proof of my reasoning, I would submit that this is the reason why spoiling a child is not a good idea. I believe a child who never has to work hard to earn anything never gets to appreciate its value because there were no experiences or lessons learned in obtaining their possessions. Thus, my examples described above clearly indicate the importance of not taking the easy way out and are directly related to the quote.

Let me share a very personal experience to illustrate the meaning of this quote, "If you find a path with no obstacles, it probably doesn't lead anywhere." I feel our most interesting experiences are connected to obstacles we have had to overcome. I know my most vivid memories are connected to challenges along the path of life and the rewards I earned as a result of these challenges. For example, when I went to Ecuador my family and I traveled into the outskirts of the Amazon Rain Forest to view the beautiful waterfalls that can be found deep within the jungle. I knew that the trip would be worth it because it would be an adventure and I would get to see breathtaking sights that most people will never see in their lifetime. However, I also understood that this would not be easy for me. For one, I knew that poisonous snakes lurk along the forest floor and that was a very real danger. My worries intensified because as we began our expedition we saw a dead snake on the ground and our guide, Jorge, explained that he had not brought the anti-venom antidote needed if someone were to be bitten. It had been left back at home base. Moreover, I had been warned that the trails were steep and muddy. My mind filled with dread because I knew we were miles away from a hospital or emergency help. To make matters worse, once we began our expedition, we would not turn back. Our only way to return to home base was to swim across the rivers of the waterfalls over huge rocks and through waters that in some spots were more than 20 feet deep. I gulped at hearing this news and my knees trembled with trepidation. I have never been a confident swimmer. The deepest water I had ever swum in was 10 feet deep and even then I was terrified. In addition, we would have to hike through an abandoned train tunnel filled with bats, in complete darkness. Can you just imagine my dread as we began our journey? My greatest obstacle of all that day can be summed up in one word—fear.

Undoubtedly, I am convinced that obstacles are needed to teach us lessons and add experiences to our lives. I say this because I had to overcome my fear that day in the rainforest and because of that I will never ever forget that experience. Fear was the enemy grabbing me by the throat and holding me back but I vanquished fear in that rainforest and I am a better person for it. I did walk down the muddy jungle floor that day and I saw flora and fauna that exists nowhere else in the world. I felt the soaking pressure of the cold rushing water on my back. I swam across four waterfalls over deep water and I was proud of myself for having accomplished that. I will forever remember the image of myself sitting on a large boulder basking in the sunlight that shone through the tree tops, while the waterfall churned and sprayed us with its mist. In that moment I felt exhaustion, pride, and awe all at once. This experience brought me closer to nature and closer to my family. Therefore, I know that overcoming this obstacle led me somewhere. If I had taken the path of no obstacle by saying I wouldn't go to the rainforest then I would never have known how brave I can be or how beautiful that rainforest and this world can be.

In conclusion, I have reflected on the meaning of the quote: "If you find a path with no obstacles, it probably leads nowhere."

In my opinion this quote suggests that problems are a reality of life and it is how we deal with these problems that teach us life lessons. As I have detailed in my essay, I firmly agree with the message of this quote. This reminds me of the expression, "no pain, no gain." That would be another way of expressing the same idea. Now go off and find the path that will lead you somewhere, I'm sure it will be a journey you won't soon forget.

Neydy Clement
Ridge Street School
Grade 6 Math and Writing Teacher

## How Does NUA Make Me Smarter?

Provides a think tank (sessions/period) where teachers can review strategies that work in the classroom.

Provides proven strategies that help me help others/students become smarter

Provides me with several principles of learning

Provides me with an overview for effective planning

Edward Howard
Maple Avenue
7th Grade Math Teacher

# How My Newark, New Jersey, NUA Cohort Makes Me Smarter

*Imagine salt and pepper. Their properties are completely different: color, taste, origin, texture, solubility and use. Yet, they are referred to most of the time as a pair, complementing each other, placed on the dining room table side by side. Salt and pepper are known in the culinary world as a duo; spices that blend to make our family dishes more flavorful.*

*The following are excerpts from the voices of students, teachers, coaches, security guards, secretaries, school lunch workers, and principals at Maple Avenue School in Newark, New Jersey as declared to their NUA mentor. Each thought, each voice, each question or statement is indicative of the school community, blending culture, learning and team teaching with an air of confidence and competence.*

*As you read the thoughts that follow, allow your mind to think in these terms: opposites are drawn to each other, people come together for common purposes, and similar minds think alike. Within the walls of Maple Avenue School, the people have become extraordinary, leaning on their sense of purpose to fulfill goals.*

*Greetings...*
*~SMILES~*
Hello Sunshine!
What a wonderful world!
You're back!!
I missed you!
Welcome!
What do you have in your bag for us today?
Hi, Ms. Neasbitt!
Ms. Neasbitt, you came back to see us!
Next time, can I help?
How come this class (team teaching demonstration) is so much better behaved than the other classes? Ms. Neasbitt, you really are a part of our family.
Listen to this lady; she has some great strategies for you!
Hi Texas!
There's the Dallas Cowboys fan...

*During the course of the site visit day...*
How do I help my students become more engaged in the lesson?
I can help my students by being a role model for them.
I need to relate my lessons more to their world.
How many times should I repeat the lesson?
I have my NUA strategies chart posted in my room.
Can I have the Five Teaching and Learning Patterns poster?
Now, who is Dr. Marks?
If I tell my students they are doing well, they succeed.
Where does Key Word Notes fit on the Pedagogical Flow Map?
My son plays football too!

How do I surface a concept from a text?

I am going to use Defining Format—that could spark a 90-minute discussion with just trying to fit the word into a category.

I used Composing With Keywords with my students and noticed more writing and better summaries.

Can you send me the Imitation Writing protocol?

Didn't you send us a Strategy Review Chart?

Can we take you to lunch?

This student really wanted to be the captain, and it shows in her writing. I can build on that strength.

I love that song. Can you play it again?

Can I copy your Strategy Review Chart?

I see you sent us a shell from the Texas coast! It was exciting to hold a part of Texas in my hand!

Did you cook collards for Thanksgiving?

I put just a bit of sugar in my cornbread.

Can you get us some NASA things for science night?

Wouldn't it be wonderful if NUA were in the entire school?  Ms. Washington and I were just discussing that the other day.

You can use List Group Label anywhere, anytime, any day.

*Goodbyes...*

Bye Ms. Neasbitt, I will miss you.

Have a good flight.

Can you bring me some cowboy boots?

When are you coming back?

Thank you for helping me see what teaching a class is like. I will never be bad in class again.

*~HUGS~*

*The presence that surrounds the NUA workshops and team teaching lessons at Maple Avenue School is one of folks committed to the Pedagogy of Confidence. Their enthusiasm, dedication, and spirit boost my work as their mentor to a higher level, instilling warmth, concern, loyalty and perseverance each time we meet. These statements guide my work. These questions illustrate a sincere yearning to learn. These remarks flow straight to my heart. I am proud, privileged, and honored to work with each and every person filling the halls of Maple Avenue School.*
*Understanding is the key...love will always conquer all.*

*I believe.*

Lisa Neasbitt
NUA Mentor

# NUA Makes the Class and Me Smarter

NUA makes the class and me smarter by allowing one to:

- Express him/herself orally, visually, intellectually, dramatically, musically, and rhythmically.

- Reinforce the Five Teaching and Learning Patterns which include:
  - Repetition
  - Recitation
  - Rituals
  - Rhythms
  - Relationship

Which have been proven effective to/in/for the retention, connection, and application of learning.

Different strategies enable a student and/or teacher to express him/herself in a multitude of ways. Since we all learn differently, the variety of strategies allows for all types of learning.

NUA actually makes learning fun!"

Alysa Schuhalker
Maple Avenue School
8th Grade Math Teacher

# Smarter

They are clay in our hands.

Do we mold them to be respectful, responsible and productive citizens?

Or

Do we beat them down with our harsh commands?

Many years from now when they look back in reflection,

Will they smile at the recollection of differentiated instruction and recall lots of praise?

Or

Will they grimace and scowl at the thought of rejection and failure they experienced during their school days?

Will they be empowered as a result of our high expectations and rigor?

Or
Are we contributing to them becoming gang bangers, drug dealers, prostitutes or the one who pulls the trigger?

Each day do we meet the challenge of our students' high demands?

Or do we just let the clay harden and slip through our hands?

We must band together, plan together and raise the bar higher.

To ensure our students' futures are brighter

And they become

Smarter.


Sharanda Evans-Pringle
Newton Street School
Literacy Coach

## Smarter...NUA

Teachers are always looking for various strategies to make teaching an exciting rewarding and productive experience for their students. I have found the answer to all our hopes and expectations, NUA!!!

I actually have the opportunity to put the strategies learned into practice and use the results to further support my teaching in the classroom.

Deborah Ballard
Maple Avenue School
8th Grade Inclusion Teacher


## The Constant Student

An odd resilience becomes manifest
As a sport coat and khaki pants clothes
A once disgruntled apathy
Residing inside the mind
Of a once lackadaisical learner

He knows the mirror does not lie
But it cannot look inside
And reveal the remnant of a student rebellious
A student who never understood the formal title
Or the process

But the process is clear now
As the image in the faculty men's room mirror

When standing in front of students
In the classroom of his nostalgia
He feels
The earnest desire he finds
In the eyes of his pupils staring
The unspoken soul cry for revelation,
Illumination, maturation
Seasoned with his history,
Discovery and style

Daniel Chojnowski
Newton Street School
Science Teacher

# Becoming Smarter...

As teachers, we are always preparing opportunities for our children to become smarter, but NUA has provided us with an opportunity to become smarter as well. The plethora of strategies that we have had an opportunity to learn, practice and perfect through our workshops, have allowed us to collaborate and support one another through teaching and learning and supporting one another through the teaching and learning process.

The NUA strategies are based on proven scientific research that has worked wonders in motivating the students to become more of a "community of learners" rather than a "group of students."

I have seen students apply strategies such as Dancing Definitions to help recall information or tests. Key Word Notes are used to help students recall and summarize text. Students create Circle Maps to organize their thoughts on a topic as a result of the thinking patterns they've acquired as a result of NUA.

In the lesson planning process it helps me become more creative getting students to recall, summarize, and apply what they have learned.

In summary, I can honestly say that the NUA strategies that we have learned have not only made my students smarter, but I have become <u>much</u> smarter as well.

Malika Moore
Maple Avenue School
7th Grade Science Teacher


# Smarter

NUA makes the students smarter by using their different strategies to organize one's learning. Learners need to be engaged in different ways of teaching because every student learns differently.

NUA teaches ways of using repetition, rhythm, recitation, etc. with teaching. It allows the students to stay involved. I have received a great support system through NUA. It has motivated me to use organizing graphics for the inclusion students. These tools help them with simplifying their activities and strengthening their intellectual performance.

Ms. Tonya Ingram
Maple Avenue School
7th Grade Inclusion Teacher

# How Has NUA Made Me Smarter?

NUA has made me smarter in the way that I teach. The rich, engaging strategies that I have learned have helped me foster connections between the students and the content.

These strategies are all research-based, so I know that I can trust them when applying them to my own lessons with my own students. Not only are these strategies effective, but they are also aligned with my own core values of creating a welcoming, culturally sensitive, and positive environment. By collaborating with my colleagues during these NUA workshops, I can see which strategies have worked in the classroom in this school. This helps me choose how best to incorporate them into my lessons.

NUA has given me the skills and knowledge to become a better teacher, and for that, I am smarter.

Jay Galbraith
Maple Avenue School
6th Grade Science Teacher


## Smarter

*Am I smarter because I teach?*
*Or*
*Are you smarter because you learn?*
*Am I smarter just because I speak?*
*Or*
*Are you smarter because you hear?*
*Literacy, Language Arts, Science, Math and more*
*Will open many a door*
*And increase your chances to explore*
*So, does it make me smarter because I teach?*
*Or*
*Does it make you even smarter because you've learned?*


Sandra F. Rolling
Dr. William H. Horton School
Teacher

# From One-Inch Dreads To Full Grown Locks

A change is gonna come
Was her thought
So she started on the top of her temple
Twist and turn she nurtures her mane
She calls them dreads started from the inch
Momma always said beware of the fashion you choose to sport
For with it comes an attitude
Dreads she calls them
She spent most of her time---engrossed in
Confrontations, altercations w/ghosts from her past---
Who sometimes appeared as shadows
silhouettes all demons who clutch
She spent hours a night casting unwanted spirits away from her space
Twisting--- and turning as she nurtured her mane
Dreads she called them---one inch and a half
She abandons many negative venerable practices
Transition is her stage---but not quite---
Limbo is her present state
Two---and a half---inches
On her way home she decides to take another route
She walks down rejects---crosses over to acceptance---
Walks-up humor then stops on the corner of truth---
The light on the corner of truth is delayed
So while there she embraces internal love
For the duration of her journey
Once home she cleans house/temple that is---trash---
She hands down nothing
Saves no unwanted mentionable---ailments---or agony
Twisting and turning cleansing and grooming
Three---and a half---inches---strong
One morning---she awakes to view her reflection
Eyes are windows to the soul wise ones once said
Slowly---pushing up lids---she surveys the soul; hers
She sees wonder-brilliant-in her original shell –
Rebuilt---faster---stronger---powerful
Twisting and turning---grooming and cleansing---
Loving and living accepting and freeing
Locks she calls them no long dreads prefix to the word
Dreadful
Lucious---full grown locks

Ms. Robin Jones, Dr. William H. Horton School, Resource Teacher

## Can We Talk?

From where I stand it seems to be so hopeless at times…….

But I trudge on because something burning…….turning inside of me won't allow me to quit…….

What is this thing that won't allow me to throw up my hands and walk away?

What do I do??????

How do I hold on???????

AHHHH……. But there is a light waaaaaay in a distance.

I can make out what it is!

Yes…….Yes…….

There it is, a hand from the back of the room…

A hand that says, "Teacher, I know the answer!"

I smile… Relieved… I can make it through another day……. I teach!

Mrs. Beverly Lambert
Grade 7 Language Arts Literacy
Dr. William H. Horton School

# How We Become Smarter Together

*Smarter is a Choice*

The classroom is alive with ideas. Each day is filled with new challenges for the students and the teacher. The teachers choose to design learning activities that let the students think and the students choose to take up those challenges and do their best. The teachers are challenged to think as the students come up with questions of their own. The students and the teachers have made the choice to be smarter.

*Smarter is a Joy*

A child filled with the joy of discovery is a delight to watch. Making a learning plan and seeing it work in the eyes and spirit of a child is a wonderful privilege.

*Smarter is a Process*

Each time we think for ourselves we are becoming who we were meant to be. As we add wisdom and understanding to our lives we realize that many times we have been wrong. As we look back at the mistakes we have made in the past, we are reminded of how far we have come. Realizing that we make mistakes keeps us humble enough to continue our search for wisdom and understanding.

*Smarter does not need a Task Master*

As we plant a bean seed and watch the tiny growing sprout, we see it struggle to break free of the hard seed coat. It was there to protect the bean before it started growing. When watching the bean sprout, it is tempting to just reach in and remove the seed coat from the sprout to speed up the process. We want to see the beautiful green leaves that are hidden beneath the coat. We want to see the leaves function as they were designed to produce their own food. In a similar way, I was impatient with my students and rushed them through their work. I told them the answers before they were ready. But as I have become smarter as a teacher I have learned to provide sunshine, nutrients, warmth and water and watch the learning happen instead of forcing it to happen. Nobody tells the plant to grow, it happens on its own under the right conditions. One day the roots will take hold and be strong enough to cause the stem and beautiful leaves inside to break free of the seed coat and start the process of photosynthesis. Our students want to think for themselves. We want to see it happen. Smarter does not need a task master.

*Smarter is Endless*

As we learn to grow in our abilities to think, we realize that we don't ever want to finish learning. Learning means we are alive.

*Smarter Together*

We are not smarter alone. Interacting, debating, and encouraging others makes us smarter together.

Mary Kay Bacallao
NUA Mentor

## The Marvelous Mass Called the Brain

Open up.
Say ahhhhhhh!

Make room in the rolodex of your mind...
Phone numbers
State capitals
Math formulas
New vocabulary
The cause of the Civil War
Birthdays and special events

Open up.
Say ahhhhhhhh!
Let the brain begin...

Making inferences
Analyzing ideas
Linking ideas and finding new clarity
Restating
Summarizing
Thinking deep thoughts

Open up.
Say ahhhhhhhh!
Allow those emotions to flow...

Pain
Love
Anger
Joy

Open up.
Say ahhhhhhhh!
Marvel at the brain that allows you to...
Walk
Talk
Hear
Feel
Think

Open up.
Say ahhhhhhhh!

Marvel at the majesty of the brain
That never runs out of storage space.

Lynn Wilhelm
NUA Mentor

A Story in Sketches by Nell Collier, NUA Mentor

Shown here are the tabby ruins at Chocolate Plantation (1789-1875), which was located at Sapelo Island, Georgia. It was once a rich antebellum Sea Island cotton plantation, built and occupied by African slaves around 1820. The name "Chocolate" was derived from the Guale Indian village Chucalate. One of the few and vanishing evidences of slavery in this country, the tabbies were constructed with sand, soil, and oyster shells. Slowly but surely, the ecosystem will expunge these reminders of early American history.

Tabby Chimney, also located on the Chocolate Plantation, is all that remains of the original plantation house erected circa 1795.

The painting "Sapelo Forest" was inspired by the quiet, lush pine forest, mottled with oak and speckled with thickets of palmetto that remain virgin, undisturbed by development. Sapelo Island is located about 65 miles south of Savannah and 5 miles off the coast of Meridian, Georgia. Only one Gullah-Geechee community remains.

Sapelo Island photographs and artwork
contributed by Patricia A. Holley,
Dr. William H. Horton Elementary School

# Index of Contributors

## Grade 6 Contributors

## Grade 6 (continued)

| | | | |
|---|---|---|---|
| Pimentel, Nicole | 51 | Sweeney, Aliyah | 28 |
| Pinto, Melissa | 16 | TaaHaa, Saalih | 21 |
| Pujois, Tania | 47 | Tarry, Delores | 47 |
| Reece, Niesha | 30 | Torres, Adrian | 40 |
| Reeves, Kayla | 15 | Torres, Danny | 59 |
| Reyes, Alexis | 39 | Toure, Ibrahima | 22 |
| Rivera, Karina | 15 | Turner, Ibreyanah | 41 |
| Rivera, Nicodemo | 45 | Ulloa, Juan Carlos | 13 |
| Rogers, Maurice | 43 | Vaquez, Esteban | 19 |
| Roselli, Lizetta | 42 | Wideman, Mikayla | 36 |
| Sabb, Tatiyana | 43 | Williams, Alea | 29 |
| Sanabria, Aiyana | 18 | Williams, Jaquan | 31 |
| Santaliz, Eddaleez | 21 | Williams, Joseily | 19 |
| Sarpong, Yaa | 24 | Williams, Tanaya | 46 |
| Sellars, Zakeeyiah | 29 | Wiltshire, Derrick | 60 |
| Selph, Kymeasha | 16 | Wolo, Rosetta | 37 |
| Shuler, Elijah Jr. | 53 | Zambrano, Julissa | 23 |
| Silva, Allondra | 7 | | |

## Grade 7 Contributors

| | | | |
|---|---|---|---|
| Acevedo, Yaideliz | 64 | Cruz, Luis | 85 |
| Amos, Katrina | 136 | Cruz, Nicholas | 115 |
| Arpaio, Alexis | 88 | Davis, Vincent | 75 |
| Arrington, Aniyah | 70 | Decen, Jeffrey | 65 |
| Avecilias, Diana | 118 | Diaz, Jordan | 104 |
| Bailey, Yahzayah | 132 | Dix, Jewelle | 125 |
| Barber, Kenneth | 91 | Dominguez, Jose | 112 |
| Bryant, Dakell | 63 | Duprey, Destiny | 75 |
| Bryant, Quiana | 101 | Fernandez-Martinez, Javier | 74 |
| Burgos, Angel | 130 | Files, Shanyah | 66 |
| Burgos, Karmin | 108 | Francis, Breyon | 135 |
| Caban, Christian | 74 | French, Jamal | 84 |
| Caldera, Cruz | 119 | Frigato, Carolina | 79 |
| Camacho, Sienna | 63 | Garcia, Damian | 82 |
| Cannon, Marques | 68 | Gillespie, QuyNay | 126 |
| Cano, Yazmira | 69 | Gillette, Ciara | 118 |
| Carson, Aneesah | 102 | Gonzalez, Daniel-John | 123 |
| Cartegena, Cristina | 128 | Gonzalez, Niasha | 113 |
| Carter, Zubaidah | 102 | Goytio, Anibal | 62 |
| Corbett, Mē Lony | 131 | Harrell, Diamante | 122 |

| | | | |
|---|---|---|---|
| Haywood, Hassan | 86 | Polanco, Mike | 134 |
| Herbert, Bashir | 132 | Polite, Daisja | 137 |
| Hernandez, Zahir | 119 | Polite, Tatyana | 124 |
| Holley, Andrea | 83 | Poneys, Lionetta | 109 |
| Holley, Phaydra | 120 | Ramirez, Maryann | 103 |
| Jacobs, Craig | 128 | Ramos, Guilherme | 104 |
| Jorden, Jordeny | 96 | Ramos, Kassandra M. | 80 |
| Lawrence, Janaiya | 96 | Rios, Kaitlyn | 67 |
| Lawson, Al-Mutokabbir | 126 | Rios, Karen | 89 |
| Levett, Anthony | 137 | Rivera, Alexis | 100 |
| Lopez, Karla | 121 | Rivera, Clary | 92 |
| Lovelock, Tom | 135 | Rivera, Nashali | 125 |
| Lyde, Jahad | 85 | Rivera, Sheina | 76 |
| Lyles, Charisma | 97 | Rodriguez, Natalie | 125 |
| Malave, Alexandra | 88 | Roopnarine, Steve | 90 |
| Maldonado, Valeria | 111 | Rosa, Ashley | 84 |
| Martin, India | 87 | Rosario, Bryan | 72 |
| Medlin, Sumayah | 130 | Rosario, Gabrielle | 71 |
| Melendez, Carmen | 103 | Santiago, Carmen | 113 |
| Mendez, Sabrina | 123 | Santiago, Gisselle | 82 |
| Mendoza, Jahaira | 110 | Santiago, Michelle | 127 |
| Menjivar, Skarleth | 112 | Simmons, Danaya | 73 |
| Miller, Isiah | 91 | Smith-Scott, Imani | 66 |
| Minier, Kelvin | 134 | Solomon, Helen | 70 |
| Molina, Jonathan | 129 | Sornza, Christopher | 109 |
| Montez, Karen | 117 | Sousa, Y'Annique | 133 |
| Moore, Llyasha | 110 | Syville, Quadir | 114 |
| Morales, Kimberly | 121 | Thomas, Basil | 122 |
| Morrison, Amber | 120 | Thompson, Kia | 117 |
| Nieves, Marcus | 111 | Toledo, Edwin | 109 |
| Nurse, Stevenson | 105 | Torres, Victor | 115 |
| Obesso, Jada | 86 | Torres, Yojana | 107 |
| Ocasio, Dayanara | 81 | Traynham, Yasmine | 68 |
| Oumarir, Ouamaima | 116 | Valentine, Michaelah | 106 |
| Peebles, Dwight | 105 | Vega, Ashley | 83 |
| Perez, Brianna | 78 | Velez, Amaris | 131 |
| Perez, John | 65 | Villegas, Luis | 133 |
| Perez, Kiana | 69 | Warren, Teliah | 101 |
| Perez, Samira | 80 | White, Shaylah | 107 |
| Pimentel, Benjamin | 64 | Williams, Jerrod | 116 |

## Grade 7 (continued)

| | | | |
|---|---|---|---|
| Williams, Robert | 72 | Zapata, Jocelyn | 76 |
| Yanez, Melissa | 124 | Zayas, Kayla-Lee | 100 |
| Yepez, Louis | 79 | Zayaz, Vaneysha | 61 |
| Young, Ha-Leem | 73 | | |

## Grade 8 Contributors

| | | | |
|---|---|---|---|
| Acevedo, Rachael | 142 | Freeman, Jibri | 138 |
| Alford, Kaylin | 159 | Gettys, Kyle | 179 |
| Alston, Jawan | 163 | Gonzalez, Onel | 163 |
| Alvarez, Francielly | 140 | Greer, Delexus | 149 |
| Anyaegbu, Cindy | 189 | Hall, Tyhiem | 172 |
| Anderson, Keisha | 177 | Hall, Zarriyah | 157 |
| Anderson, Tarence | 158 | Hammond, Khasheem S. | 174 |
| Ballo, Ferima | 176 | Hardy, Briana | 152 |
| Banks, Ciera | 168 | Harris, Precious | 187 |
| Barber, Donna | 191 | Hawthorne, Shantell | 176 |
| Battles, Melissa | 155 | Hayes, Jerry | 164 |
| Benson, Joshua | 175 | Horace, Iijhane T. | 153 |
| Bey, Denzel | 154 | Hunt, Anthony | 149 |
| Brinkley, Lavonte | 177 | Issac, Bevon | 165 |
| Brown, Nafi | 184 | Jackson, Samyra | 157 |
| Brumfield, Amber | 190 | Jennings, Ayaad | 181 |
| Burks, Mecca | 167 | Johnson, Clifton | 164 |
| Burris, Ebony | 160 | Jones, Ayannah | 160 |
| Burwell Dayvon | 150 | Knight, Davon | 178 |
| Butler, Hyshawn | 165 | Lawson, Ashanta | 179 |
| Carson, Ameerah | 140 | Logan, Brianna | 150 |
| Conover, Nahla | 188 | McCann, Troy | 154 |
| Cuevas, Thayris | 156 | Mcclendon, Dasjavel | 183 |
| Cunningham, Amani | 161 | McCray, Shanna | 185 |
| Daniels, DeJuan | 193 | McKinney, Ahquillah | 152 |
| Daughtridge, Zhane | 183 | McKinney, Tynasia | 142 |
| Davis, Laquan | 153 | McKnight, Ayanna | 182 |
| Dejesus, Karol | 144 | McLean, Kevona | 182 |
| DeLeon, Carlos | 178 | Meggett, Jarvis | 186 |
| Dormevil, Mytasia | 181 | Mensah-Boateng, Rosslin | 155 |
| Fauntleroy, Kijana | 178 | Mohammed, Sheerise | 168 |
| Fermin, Albin | 139 | Mora, Karina | 148 |

## Grade 8 (continued)

| | | | |
|---|---|---|---|
| Morel, Pablo | 143 | Smith, Tamadg | 180 |
| Motiram, Sachin | 175 | Smith, Ty'Tiana | 147 |
| Moultrie, Marsellas | 174 | Smith, Tyanna | 141 |
| Mount, Jiovanna | 172 | Soto, Leslie A. | 143 |
| Muhammad, Halimah | 140 | Stevens, Eyonnie | 189 |
| Neal, Tyrrie | 188 | Stevens, Ibn | 171 |
| Olmo, Ashley | 187 | Stevenson, Jasmine | 184 |
| Ordonez, Roger | 170 | Stewart, Sameerah | 169 |
| Owens, Akeem | 185 | Teran, Alicia | 146 |
| Paul, Tamara | 191 | Thomas, Deandre | 141 |
| Perry, Jawan | 165 | Thomas, Lexus | 171 |
| Pickett, Rahsaan | 151 | Thompson, Shaneyrah | 148 |
| Pillay, Nalita | 145 | Tillman, Timothy | 168 |
| Pirapakaran, Brian | 158 | Valentin, Joshua | 192 |
| Plush-Williams, Ronnay | 167 | Vasquez, Roberto | 173 |
| Quinones, Nigere | 159 | Wah, Honoriah | 140 |
| Reyes, Joseph | 186 | Washington, Tanaysia | 180 |
| Rivera, Reinaldo | 139 | Williams, Keiana | 173 |
| Rosa, Joe-seph A. | 151 | Wilson, Elaine | 169 |
| Rushing, Keearah | 147 | Yancey, Eric | 162 |
| Santiago, Felix | 183 | Yaport, Gabriel | 170 |
| Simmons, Dashaun | 166 | Younger, Jasmine | 166 |

## Adult Contributors

| | | | |
|---|---|---|---|
| Bacallao, Mary Kay | 210 | Hunter, Kakila | 194 |
| Ballard, Deborah | 205 | Ingram, Tonya | 206 |
| Chojnowski, Daniel | 205 | Jackson, Yvette | 2 |
| Clement, Neydy | 198 | Jones, Robin | 208 |
| Collier, Nell | 212 | Lambert, Beverly | 209 |
| Cooper, Eric | 3 | Lichten, Matthew | 195 |
| Currey, Lydia | 196 | Moore, Malika | 206 |
| Evans-Pringle, Sharanda | 204 | Neasbitt, Lisa | 201 |
| Galbraith, Jay | 207 | Rolling, Sandra F. | 207 |
| Haygood, Charity | 197 | Schuhalker, Alysa | 203 |
| Holley, Patricia A. | 213 | Wilhelm, Lynn | 211 |
| Howard, Edward | 200 | Wise, Andrea | 4 |

# Discussion Questions for Teachers and Students

What do you like best about the publication?

What is your favorite poem? Why do you like that one the best?

What is your favorite story? Why do you like that one the best?

What is your favorite essay? Why do you like that one the best?

What is your favorite drawing? Why do you like that one the best?

Are there any questions you would like to ask the writers and artists?

Would you like to contribute to a publication like this if we were to do one next year? What would you want to contribute?

What are some things you would want to remember to do if you created something for a publication like this?

Made in the USA
Charleston, SC
18 April 2010